FAIRYTALE FOOD

Published by Preface 2012

10 9 8 7 6 5 4 3 2 1

First published in Great Britain in 2012 by Preface Publishing

20 Vauxhall Bridge Road
London, SW1V 2SA

An imprint of The Random House Group Limited

www.randomhouse.co.uk
www.prefacepublishing.co.uk

Addresses for companies within The Random House Group Limited
can be found at www.randomhouse.co.uk

The Random House Group Limited Reg. No. 954009

A CIP catalogue record for this book is available from the British Library

ISBN 978 1 84809 357 7

Designed by Two Associates
Printed and bound in China by C&C Offset Printing Co. Ltd

FAIRYTALE FOOD

 LUCIE CASH

❧❦❧

ILLUSTRATIONS BY
YELENA BRYKSENKOVA

preface

To My Family

YOU KNOW WHO YOU ARE

CONTENTS

Belle and her Beau

Beauty and the Beast Burgers
(Beauty's Plucky Chicken Burgers, Beast's Best Beef Burgers) 56
Pretty Sweet Potatoes 59
Devoted Dips (Faithful Blue Cheese, Beloved Barbecue Sauce,
Doting Garlic and Chive Mayo) 60
True Love's Hearts 62

Fairy Folk

Enchanted Forest Gateau 66
Fairy Chocolate Cups 68
Goblin Granitas 71

Off to Neverland

Peter Pancakes (Smoked Salmon and Cream Cheese,
Bacon and Mushroom, Spinach and Ricotta) 74
Captain Hook's Fish Pie 78
Jolly Roger Jelly 81
Tinkerbell's Trifle 82

I'll Huff and I'll Puff

Three Little Pigs in Blankets 86
Huff 'n' Puff Pork 88
Piggy No. 1's Apple Sauce 89
The Wolf's Sticky Ribs 91

CONTENTS

 Not a Teddy Bear's Picnic

 Wonderland

 Damsels and Dragons

Introduction

Once upon a time, a young(ish) maiden decided that she was fed up with cooking the same old beans on toast and pasta bakes every night; she longed for some magic and sparkle in her cooking. One day she left her cosy cottage (flat in West London), pen and paper in hand, and travelled to find some of the most inspirational cooks of all time; she went to the land of Fairytales.

The maiden travelled for months, visiting her most-loved fairytale characters; some were wonderfully sweet and generous, others were a bit grumpy and a little scary, but they all gave her ideas, tips and the confidence to create her own delicious recipes.

The maiden returned home with her beautiful book, filled with the precious recipes and the memories of the characters she had met along the way. The book was passed from generation to generation, treasured by all who owned it; and now, dear reader, I am passing it on to you.

The Rules
of
FAIRYTALE COOKING

Ensure that your cauldron is sparkling clean!

When stirring, always stir widdershins (counter-clockwise); Snow White advised against this technique, as she said it was only ever used by witches to stir their wicked brews, but according to her stepmother this technique is used by all sorts of enchanted folk, not just witches, and is perfectly safe. It is also said to sometimes summon the power of the fairies, so it can't be all bad.

Check your kitchen thoroughly for signs of goblins (little footprints, sticky fingermarks). Goblins are notoriously mischievous creatures and relish any opportunity to cause chaos. They have taken a particularly strong liking to kitchens in recent times, as the ever more complex layouts and storage compartments provide them with plenty of elaborate hiding places.

Fairytale cooking is good-looking cooking.
Make sure you are stocked up on all things
colourful, glittery, twinkly and sparkly
and you'll be well prepared when you
come to decorate your creations.

Fairy dust (well, edible glitter) is a must-use
item when embellishing your baked delights.
Thanks to the commercial know-how of a few
high-flying fairies, it is not only affordable but also
widely available in a variety of beautiful colours.

Finally, the key to being an
enchanting fairytale cook is having
fun and being inspired; it's not about
having magical cooking powers. As
long as you are happy and enjoying
yourself, your food will be as
delightful as you are.

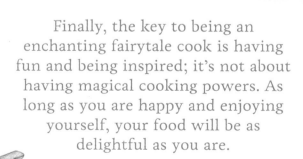

WHO
IS THE
fairest
OF THEM
ALL
?

Seven Dwarf Salad

Evil Stepmother's Stew

Snow White's Apple Tart

Blood Red Velvet Cake

'Snow White's stepmother was a nightmare; she was trying to poison the stew!'

Seven Dwarf Salad

The Seven Dwarves were Snow White's little knights in shining armour – they kept her as safe and as sound as they could, hidden away from her wicked stepmother, and in return she did a bit of cleaning, cooking and washing up for them in order to pay her way. However, Snow White noticed that the dwarves weren't the biggest eaters of fruit and vegetables; they told her they were dreary and boring so they didn't bother with them. Spotting a challenge, Snow White decided to make a salad so full of goodies that not even the most disgruntled salad-shirking dwarf could resist. For all you lettuce-dodgers out there, here is Snow White's recipe for a delicious mixed salad; it's fresh, colourful and flavoursome – enjoy!

SERVES 4–6

1 x 200g bag of mixed
   salad leaves
5 spring onions, finely
   chopped
2 large tomatoes, finely
   chopped
¼ of a cucumber, sliced
1 green pepper, sliced
1 yellow pepper, sliced
8–10 radishes, sliced
2–3 sticks of celery,
   finely chopped
1 large carrot, peeled
   and grated
1 x 198g tin of sweetcorn,
   drained and rinsed
1 x 220g tin of chickpeas,
   drained and rinsed

To create your salad, all you need to do is prepare the vegetables, chopping and slicing everything up so it's nice and fine, then put all the ingredients into a large pretty salad bowl and mix them together. That's it.

You can of course add or replace some of these ingredients to suit you, and serve it with some salad dressing or good-quality mayonnaise. I particularly like making this salad for parties and barbecues so everyone can just dig in, but it's also wonderful served alongside cold cuts, some hunks of cheese and a steaming hot dish of buttered Jersey Royals – delicious!

Mirror, Mirror on the Wall

Evil Stepmother's Stew

Fairytale Land seems to be riddled with evil stepmothers. Usually they are depicted as downright murderous and duplicitous women who want nothing more than to see their stepchildren suffer or disappear entirely! I feel a tad sorry for Snow White's stepmother; did anyone ever stop to think how she felt having to compete with an overly perfect stepdaughter who was the apple of her father's eye and, to top it off, the most beautiful woman in the entire world? It's enough to make anyone jealous with rage. Anyway, love her or loathe her, this particular stepmother happens to make a very hearty venison stew (without poison, I promise); an essential dish for an autumnal evening.

SERVES 4–6

1–2 tablespoons olive oil, for frying

1kg diced venison

2 large onions, peeled and roughly chopped

salt and freshly ground black pepper

6 large carrots, peeled and cut into large chunks

1 tablespoon mushroom ketchup

a handful of fresh flat-leaf parsley, roughly chopped

2 bay leaves

3 tablespoons tomato purée

approx. 1 litre beef stock (just enough to cover the meat and vegetables)

1. Preheat the oven to 190°C/170°C fan/gas mark 5.

2. In a large pan (or a casserole dish that can be used on the hob as well as in the oven), heat the olive oil and brown the pieces of venison in batches, placing them aside in a bowl once browned.

3. Turn the heat down to low and add the onions to the pan with a pinch of salt so that they don't stick. Cook for a few minutes, until they soften and become translucent.

4. Add the carrots, mushroom ketchup, parsley and bay leaves, then return the venison to the pan. Add the tomato purée, season with salt and pepper and give it all a good stir.

5. Add enough beef stock to just cover the meat and vegetables. Increase the heat and bring the stew to a simmer.

6. Remove from the heat and place a dampened circle of baking parchment (a cartouche) into the pan so that it just covers the top of the stew – this will allow it to cook gently in the oven and reduce down without burning on top.

7. Place in the oven and leave to cook for a good 2½–3 hours, until the sauce has reduced right down and the meat is meltingly tender.

8. I like to serve this stew with hunks of crusty bread, but it is just as good with new potatoes and some buttered greens on the side.

Snow White's Apple Tart

*Despite her angelic appearance, satin-faced Snow White can, I hear, be a little bit flirtatious . . .
I suppose we can all be when the moment takes us! And well, why shouldn't she? It's nice to see
her adding a bit of blusher to her alabaster cheeks and letting her ebony locks down for once;
she is the fairest, after all, so why not flaunt it? This cheeky apple and caramel tart is made in
Snow White's honour – it's beautiful, sweet and just as fruity as she is. Delve in!*

SERVES 6–8

Pastry

200g plain flour
a pinch of salt
100g cold unsalted butter,
    cut into dice, plus a little
    for greasing
1 large egg, beaten
a little water, if needed

Filling

25g unsalted butter
450g baking apples,
    peeled, cored and cut
    into small chunks
25g caster sugar
1 tablespoon water
2 teaspoons Amaretto
½ tablespoon lemon juice
1 x 397g tin of caramel
    (I use Carnation)

Topping

1 medium eating apple
1 tablespoon lemon juice
½ teaspoon caster sugar
½ teaspoon ground cinnamon

1. Lightly grease a 23cm flan dish with a little butter and set
   to one side.

2. To make the pastry, place the flour and salt in a large bowl
   with the butter and then, using your fingers, rub the butter
   into the flour until you have a mixture that resembles
   breadcrumbs. Add the egg and, still using your hands, bring
   the mixture together to form a dough – add a little water if it's
   too dry. Place the ball of dough into a polythene bag and pop it
   into the fridge for about 30 minutes to firm up.

3. Preheat the oven to 200°C/180°C fan/gas mark 6. When the
   pastry has rested, roll it out on a floured work surface and
   place it in your prepared flan dish. Prick the base with a fork,
   then cover with baking parchment and baking beans and
   blind bake in the oven. After about 10 minutes, remove the
   parchment and baking beans and return the flan dish to the
   oven for a further 5 minutes to enable the base to dry out
   a little. Remove from the oven and leave to one side to
   cool slightly.

4. Next, make the apple filling. In a large non-stick pan, melt
   the butter and add the apples, caster sugar, water, Amaretto
   and lemon juice. Cook over a medium heat for about 10–15
   minutes, until the apples are soft and there is no liquid left.
   Take off the heat and leave to cool.

5. Leaving the skin on, slice the eating apple into fine half-moons
   and place in a small dish with the lemon juice – this will
   prevent the apples turning brown.

6. Next, scoop the caramel out of the can straight into the pastry case – smooth all over the base to get an even layer. Spoon the cooked apples on top of the caramel and smooth with a palette knife. Finally, decorate the top of the tart with the slices of eating apple and sprinkle the top with a little caster sugar and cinnamon.

7. Return the tart to the oven for another 20–25 minutes, so that the pastry is fully cooked through. Remove from the oven and leave to cool completely before popping it into the fridge. I think this tart is best served chilled, so remove it from the fridge about 10 minutes before serving. I can quite happily eat this on its own, but it goes wonderfully with cream or custard.

Blood Red Velvet Cake

Having naturally beautiful, plump, ruby red lips is probably what most women dream of. For one thing it would mean never needing to buy lipstick ever again, and, even better, avoiding the guaranteed embarrassment of a pillar-box smear of red either just below the nose or on the front teeth! I don't think Snow White realized how lucky she was with her perfect scarlet pout. This stunningly rosy red velvet cake is deepest crimson, and filled with sumptuous raspberries and rose-scented cream it's guaranteed to put a smile on anyone's lips.

SERVES 8–10

Cake batter
250g plain flour, sifted
2 tablespoons cocoa powder
½ teaspoon salt
120g softened unsalted butter
250g caster sugar
2 large eggs
1 teaspoon vanilla extract
240ml buttermilk
½ teaspoon red food
  colouring paste
1 teaspoon bicarbonate of soda
1 teaspoon vinegar

Filling and topping
300ml double cream
½ tablespoon caster sugar
1½ teaspoons rosewater
500g fresh raspberries

To decorate
plain chocolate (optional)
white edible glitter (optional)

1. Preheat the oven to 190°C/170°C fan/gas 5, and grease and line 2 x 20cm round cake tins.

2. Sift the flour, cocoa powder and salt into a large mixing bowl and set aside.

3. In another large bowl, cream the butter and sugar together until smooth, pale and fluffy, using an electric hand whisk or mixer. Add the eggs, one at a time, stirring well after each addition. Stir in the vanilla extract.

4. Mix the buttermilk and the food colouring paste together in a measuring jug.

5. Pour a third of the buttermilk/colouring mixture into the creamed butter and sugar, and beat well until combined. Then add a third of the flour/cocoa powder and beat well. Repeat this process until all the buttermilk and flour have been incorporated and you have a smooth and even mixture.

6. Next, in a small cup, combine the bicarbonate of soda and vinegar and fold into the cake batter.

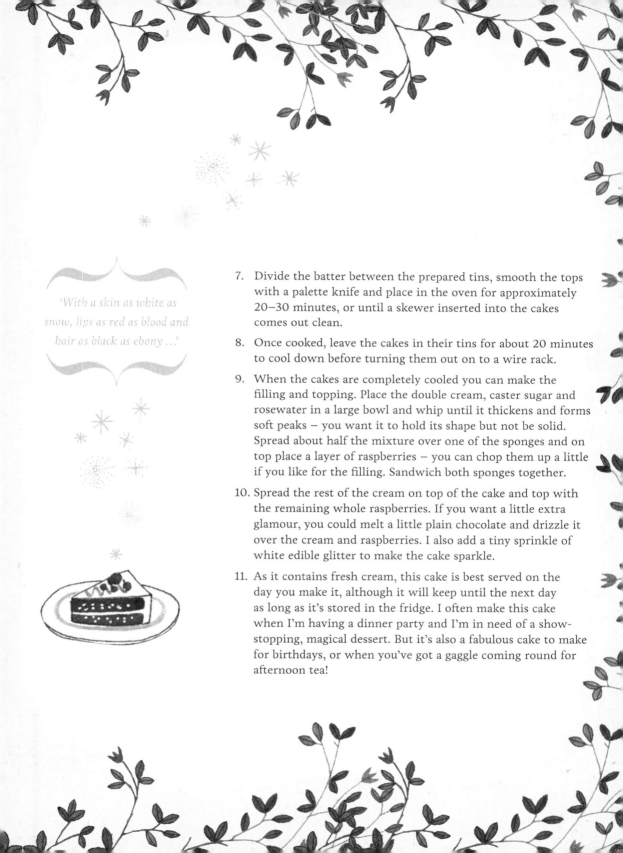

'With a skin as white as snow, lips as red as blood and hair as black as ebony ...'

7. Divide the batter between the prepared tins, smooth the tops with a palette knife and place in the oven for approximately 20–30 minutes, or until a skewer inserted into the cakes comes out clean.

8. Once cooked, leave the cakes in their tins for about 20 minutes to cool down before turning them out on to a wire rack.

9. When the cakes are completely cooled you can make the filling and topping. Place the double cream, caster sugar and rosewater in a large bowl and whip until it thickens and forms soft peaks – you want it to hold its shape but not be solid. Spread about half the mixture over one of the sponges and on top place a layer of raspberries – you can chop them up a little if you like for the filling. Sandwich both sponges together.

10. Spread the rest of the cream on top of the cake and top with the remaining whole raspberries. If you want a little extra glamour, you could melt a little plain chocolate and drizzle it over the cream and raspberries. I also add a tiny sprinkle of white edible glitter to make the cake sparkle.

11. As it contains fresh cream, this cake is best served on the day you make it, although it will keep until the next day as long as it's stored in the fridge. I often make this cake when I'm having a dinner party and I'm in need of a show-stopping, magical dessert. But it's also a fabulous cake to make for birthdays, or when you've got a gaggle coming round for afternoon tea!

CLIMBING *the* BEANSTALK

Poor Woman's Barley Broth

Poor Man's Dinner

Jack's Magic Bean Salad

The Giant's Steak Pie

'The Giant is such a charmer and not half as scary as Jack makes out. A lot of fuss about nothing if you ask me, he's a right old softie!'

Poor Woman's Barley Broth

Like dear young Jack's poverty-stricken mother, there are moments when we all need to keep an eye on the pennies – so why not cook up something that's warm and hearty to eat, without spending every last precious bean! This vegetable broth is both a cheap and a healthy option, plus it's tasty, filling and wholesome; just what one needs before hitting the shops . . .

SERVES 2–4

1 small knob of butter or
   1 tablespoon of olive oil,
   for frying
1 medium onion,
   finely chopped
2 sticks of celery, cut into
   small chunks
1 large carrot, cut into
   small chunks
100g baby button
   mushrooms, halved
½ tablespoon
   mushroom ketchup
100g pearl barley
1 bay leaf
1 litre chicken stock
   (homemade or shop-bought,
   either is fine)
1 x 410g tin of flageolet beans,
   drained and rinsed well
200g mangetout or sugar
   snaps, halved
salt and freshly ground
   black pepper

1. In a large pan, melt the butter and fry the onions over a medium heat for a few minutes until they have softened. Add the celery and carrots and fry for a few more minutes, letting the vegetables gently sweat down.

2. Next, add the button mushrooms along with the mushroom ketchup and cook for 2–3 minutes.

3. Stir in the pearl barley, add the bay leaf and pour in the stock. Bring the broth to the boil, then turn the heat down, cover and leave to simmer for 1–1½ hours, until the barley is tender.

4. When the barley is cooked, add the flageolet beans and the mangetout or sugar snaps; the beans and peas need to just cook through, you don't want them to overcook and become mushy. Season well with salt and pepper.

5. Serve in bowls, with a hunk of crusty bread on the side.

TIP

You could of course decide on your own choice of vegetables, depending on what you prefer, and although I generally use homemade chicken stock, you could use vegetable stock instead – just make sure it's a good one.

Poor Man's Dinner

Do you ever get home from work, pop your slippers on, wander into the kitchen, open your cupboards and just sigh . . .? There's nothing but some spuds and an onion in there, languishing and looking a tiny bit sad. And to top it off, you don't have enough money in your purse for a takeaway. Not very inspiring, is it? Well, Jack's great-granny would have danced a little jig at such a discovery, as these unassuming vegetables are the key ingredients for this, her cheap and very cheerful dinnertime dish. With layers of potato, onion, crispy bacon lardons and a cheesy topping, this is a tasty and hearty supper for anyone watching the pennies: the perfect poor man's dinner!

SERVES 4

olive oil

200g pancetta or bacon lardons (if they have a thick rind, trim it off)

750g potatoes, peeled and finely sliced

1 large onion, cut into rings

½ teaspoon dried sage

freshly ground black pepper

½–1 tablespoon butter

150ml milk

75g Cheddar cheese, grated

1. Preheat the oven to 200°C/180°C fan/gas mark 6 and lightly grease the inside of a casserole dish (preferably one with a lid) with a little olive oil.

2. In a small non-stick pan, fry the little lardons of pancetta or bacon until they are crisp – you don't need any oil, as they will easily cook in their own fat. Once they are cooked, remove them from the pan and place them on some kitchen paper to soak up the excess fat.

3. Now begin to layer up your dish. Start off by placing a layer of potatoes at the bottom, then a layer of onion, and scatter some of the lardons on top. Sprinkle with a little sage and some pepper (I don't add salt, as I find the pancetta/bacon provides enough seasoning), then repeat the process until all the ingredients are used up and you are left with a final layer of potatoes on top. Season with a little more pepper and dot little knobs of the butter randomly over the potatoes. Finally, pour in the milk, pop a lid on the casserole and place in the oven.

4. After 45 minutes remove the lid, check that the potatoes are cooked through (you can do this by just poking them with a sharp knife), then return the dish to the oven for a further 10 minutes so that the top can start to brown. When the 10 minutes are up, scatter the grated Cheddar on top and finish off in the oven for a further 5 minutes, until the cheese has melted and the top is golden.

5. I like to serve my poor man's dinner with some simple vegetables: a spoonful or three of garden peas or some steamed broccoli are my favourites.

Jack's Magic Bean Salad

I think it's fair to say that we can all suffer from slight bouts of retail madness. I'd put Jack's frivolous sale of the family cow for a handful of beans down to just that; he was tempted and persuaded, and who could blame him? To be honest, wouldn't we all do the same for some brightly coloured beans – better having those in the house than a cow . . . Fortunately for Jack they turned out to be pretty lucrative little beans, and he and his mother became rich beyond their wildest dreams. I don't think this bean salad will make anyone a billionaire, but it is a lovely, light summery side dish.

SERVES 2

1 tomato, finely chopped
½ a shallot, finely chopped
1 spring onion, finely chopped
1 stick of celery, finely chopped
1 x 410g tin of mixed bean
    salad, drained and rinsed well
    (you could use a tin of
    cannellini beans if you prefer)
a squeeze of lemon juice
½ tablespoon extra virgin
    olive oil
1 teaspoon white wine vinegar
salt and freshly ground
    black pepper

1. Put the chopped vegetables into a bowl with the beans and mix well.

2. Add the lemon juice, olive oil and vinegar and stir, making sure all the beans and vegetables are coated in the dressing.

3. Lastly, season to taste with salt and pepper.

TIP

If you want to turn this salad into a magical dish for lunch, you could add some tuna or cooked chicken.

31

The Giant's Steak Pie

I am completely unashamed when I say that I love a good pie – there is no point in denial!
If you need to satisfy the most giant of appetites, this pie will do the trick. It always goes down
a treat with members of my family, who can never resist a second or third slice.
No Englishman's bones are used in this recipe.

SERVES 4–6

Shortcrust pastry

225g plain flour

a pinch of salt

110g cold butter

approx. 2–3 tablespoons
   cold water

1 large egg, beaten

Filling

½ tablespoon olive oil,
   for frying

1kg braising steak, cut into
   2cm cubes

2 onions, roughly chopped

salt and freshly ground
   black pepper

300g button mushrooms,
   halved

2 teaspoons
   mushroom ketchup

2 teaspoons
   Worcestershire sauce

1 tablespoon plain flour

600ml good-quality beef stock

2 bay leaves

To make the filling:

1. I would advise making the pie filling a day in advance –
   it takes a good couple of hours to cook and must be completely
   cold when it goes into the pastry. If you put the filling in hot,
   your pie will suffer from a soggy bottom and that just
   won't do.

2. Heat the oil in a large pan on a high heat and brown the cubes
   of beef in batches, placing them aside in a bowl once done.

3. Turn the heat down to a moderate level and fry the onions in
   the meaty juices until they start to soften. If you find they are
   starting to stick to the pan or catch, add a little salt.

4. Next, add the mushrooms, mushroom ketchup and
   Worcestershire sauce and cook for a few minutes.

5. Return the beef to the pan and add the flour – make sure that
   all the meat and vegetables are coated in the flour. Then start
   to add the stock, stirring as you go to ensure that all the flour
   is incorporated – this will make gloriously thick pie gravy.

6. Add the bay leaves and season well with salt and pepper. Bring
   to the boil, then turn the heat right down and let the filling
   gently simmer on the hob for a good 2 hours or so, until the
   beef is meltingly tender and the gravy has thickened and
   reduced. When cooked, leave the filling to cool completely.

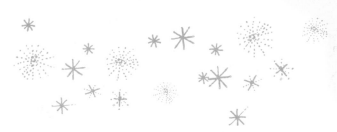

*'Fee-fi-fo-fum, I smell the
blood of an Englishman.
Be he alive or be he dead,
I'll grind his bones to make
my bread.'*

To make the pastry:

7. Place the flour and salt in a large bowl and rub in the butter to form a crumbly mixture.

8. Add the water a spoonful at a time, stirring it well into the mixture – you may need more or less water than I've suggested here, so just add it gradually until you can bring the dough together with your hands.

9. Divide the dough into 2 balls, wrap them in clingfilm or place them in polythene bags, and put them into the fridge for about 30 minutes to firm up.

10. As this pie has a top and a bottom you'll need to roll out the bottom layer of pastry first, put it into your pie dish and blind bake it in the oven at 210°C/190°C fan/gas mark 6½ for about 20 minutes, until it is golden brown. Once cooked leave it to cool down.

11. Once cooled, add the filling, then roll out the remaining pastry and top the pie, crimping the edges to seal. Trim any excess pastry from the sides and brush the top of the pie with beaten egg – this will give it a gorgeous golden colour when it's cooked.

12. When you're ready to cook the pie, preheat the oven to 210°C/190°C fan/gas mark 6½ and bake it for 30–40 minutes, until the pastry and filling are thoroughly cooked through.

13. Once cooked, let the pie stand for about 5 minutes before cutting it. I like to serve it with mashed or boiled potatoes and some garden peas.

AWOKEN
with
A
KISS

Sleeping Beauty Bites

Bad Fairy Cakes

Prince Charming's Kisses

'I visited the Bad Fairy this morning; she was on her best behaviour but I didn't hang around, she is evil after all and cannot be trusted with that spindle.'

Sleeping Beauty Bites ✳

A little-known fact about Sleeping Beauty is that before she fell foul of the cursed spindle, she was actually quite a party animal. Rumour has it that the fateful incident occurred at one of her late-night bashes. She went upstairs to touch up her lipstick, and, having consumed a fair amount of rosé on an empty stomach, she tripped over her bedroom rug and pricked her finger on the spinning wheel she'd used that morning to repair her party dress. In a funny sort of way the curse must have done her some good – after all, she did have a hundred years to sleep off her hangover. You'll be pleased to hear that, now fully conscious, she still hosts the odd party but ensures that there are plenty of tasty tummy-lining nibbles to go around . . . and of course, there's not a spinning wheel in sight!

Sleepy Salmon Pâté

SERVES 6–8

235g smoked salmon
1 tablespoon lemon juice
230g low-fat cream cheese
salt and freshly ground
  black pepper
toast and lemon wedges,
  to serve

1. Put the salmon into a food processor and blitz for a few seconds until it's finely chopped.

2. Add the lemon juice and cream cheese and blitz again until you have a well-blended mixture – it doesn't have to be perfectly smooth. Season with a little salt and pepper to taste – I find it doesn't need much.

3. Pop the pâté into one bowl if everyone's sharing and spoon into little ramekins if they're not!

4. Serve with some fresh crusty bread or toast, with some wedges of lemon on the side.

Magic Mini-Quiches

1 x 375g pack of ready-rolled
  shortcrust pastry
1 teaspoon olive oil
125g chestnut mushrooms,
  finely chopped
salt and freshly ground black
  pepper
a bunch of fresh chives about
  the width of your finger
1 large whole egg, plus 1 large
  egg yolk
75ml double cream
30g Cheddar cheese, grated

TIP

Normally I am all for making my
own pastry, but I just find it so
much easier to use ready-rolled
pastry for party food like this – it
takes the pressure off when time
is of the essence. You can also
experiment a bit with different
fillings for your quiches; a little
bit of fried onion and tomato
with cheese on top is another of
my favourites, but you can be as
adventurous (or not) as you like!

1. Preheat the oven to 200°C/180°C fan/gas mark 6 and lightly
    grease and flour 2 x 24-hole mini muffin trays.

2. Take your sheet of pastry and lay it on a board. Using a 5cm
    round cutter, cut out 24 discs of pastry and place them into
    the holes of your muffin trays. Blind bake in the oven for 10
    minutes, then remove and leave to one side.

3. Heat the olive oil in a small pan and fry the chopped
    mushrooms over a medium heat until they are cooked
    through; this should take about 5–10 minutes. Season well
    with salt and pepper.

4. Once the mushrooms are cooked, spoon about half a teaspoon
    of them into each pastry case until they are all used up. Next,
    snip the chives and sprinkle some on top of the mushrooms.

5. Put the whole egg into a bowl with the extra yolk and beat
    well. Add the double cream and give the mixture a good whisk.
    Season well with salt and pepper.

6. Using a teaspoon, gently spoon the cream mixture into each of
    the pastry cases, making sure not to overfill them but ensuring
    that the mushroom filling is just covered.

7. Finally sprinkle a little grated Cheddar on the top of each
    mini-quiche and return them to the oven for about 10–15
    minutes, until the quiche filling has puffed a little and is
    golden brown. Keep an eye on them so they don't burn!

8. When ready, remove the mini-quiches from the oven and leave
    them to cool slightly before taking them out of their trays.
    I think they are best served at room temperature – they make
    the perfect bite-sized nibble for any party!

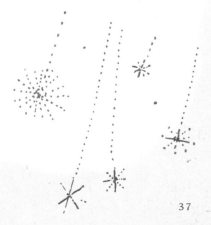

Beauty's Bruschettas

MAKES 24 MINI-
BRUSCHETTAS — IF YOU
NEED MORE FOR A LARGER
GATHERING, JUST DOUBLE
UP THE QUANTITIES!

1 x 400g can of
   chopped tomatoes
2 teaspoons balsamic vinegar
salt and freshly ground
   black pepper
½ a French stick, cut into
   24 slices about 2cm thick
   (the bread should just be
   going stale — if it's not, slice
   it up in advance and leave it
   to dry out for a few hours)
2 tablespoons olive oil
   (use a good one)
1 large garlic clove
a small bunch of fresh basil

1. Preheat the oven to 220°C/200°C fan/gas mark 7.

2. Put the chopped tomatoes into a non-stick pan with the balsamic vinegar, salt and pepper, and cook on a medium heat for about 10 minutes, until the tomatoes have reduced down and thickened. Taste and add more seasoning if necessary, then remove from the heat and leave to one side.

3. Place the slices of bread on a large baking sheet and place in the oven for a couple of minutes to gently warm through.

4. Remove from the oven and brush each slice with a little olive oil. Next, take the garlic clove, cut it in half lengthways, and rub the cut sides over each slice.

5. Put back into the oven for another 4–5 minutes, until the bread just starts to dry out, then remove and spread about a heaped teaspoon of the tomatoes on to each slice.

6. Return the bruschettas to the oven for a further 5 minutes, until they are crispy and golden.

7. Finally, top each one with a fresh basil leaf. Serve warm from the oven on a large platter and watch everyone dig in!

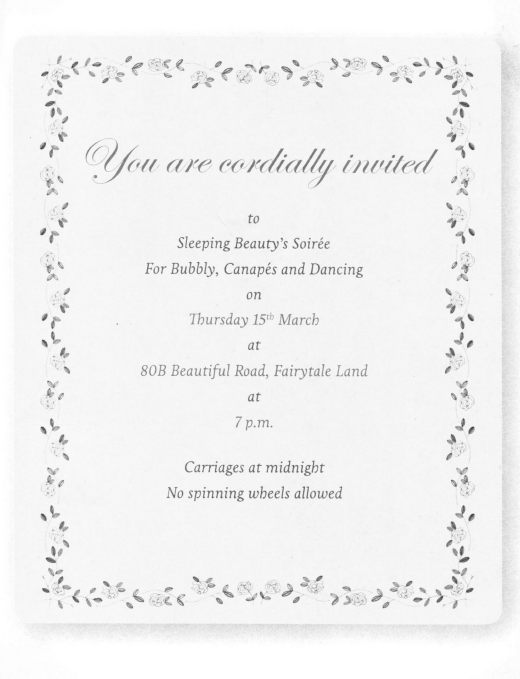

You are cordially invited

to

Sleeping Beauty's Soirée

For Bubbly, Canapés and Dancing

on

Thursday 15th March

at

80B Beautiful Road, Fairytale Land

at

7 p.m.

Carriages at midnight

No spinning wheels allowed

Bad Fairy Cakes ✳

The Bad Fairy is undoubtedly malevolent, wicked and particularly fond of curses involving spinning wheels . . . well, aren't we all occasionally? In a tribute to our dark side, these chocolate cupcakes are sumptuous, rich and, yes, OK, just a tiny bit bad for us. How naughty!

MAKES 12

Cake batter

110g softened unsalted butter
110g caster sugar
2 large eggs
110g self-raising flour
2 tablespoons cocoa powder
1 teaspoon baking powder
a pinch of salt
2 tablespoons milk

Filling

2 x 290g tins of blackcurrants
   in fruit juice (choose ones
   with no added sugar)
2 teaspoons caster sugar

Icing

100g plain chocolate
1 tablespoon caster sugar
2 tablespoons soured cream

To decorate

dark chocolate buttons
   (optional)
red edible glitter (optional)

1. Preheat the oven to 190°C/170°C fan/gas mark 5 and fill a 12-hole muffin tray with paper muffin cases.

2. Cream the butter and caster sugar together until pale and fluffy, then add the eggs one at a time, mixing well.

3. Sift the flour, cocoa powder, baking powder and salt into a bowl and add to the egg mixture a third at a time, along with the milk, mixing well to ensure that all the dry and wet ingredients are combined.

4. Spoon the mixture into the muffin tray, filling the paper cases about two-thirds full. Place in the centre of the oven and bake for about 20 minutes, until the tops are springy to touch, or a skewer comes out clean. Leave the cakes to cool on a wire rack.

5. To make the tangy blackcurrant filling, drain the tinned blackcurrants but save about 1 tablespoon of the juice. Put the fruit and the saved juice into a food processor or blender, add the sugar and blitz quickly until pulped – the mixture doesn't have to be smooth. Taste, and add a little more sugar if you feel it is too tart. I like the filling to be quite sharp so that it contrasts nicely with the sweetness of the sponge cake.

6. Once the cakes are completely cooled, angle a small sharp knife and cut a round out of the middle of each cake, leaving a hole in the centre. Cut the rounds in half (to make fairy wings) and set aside. Fill the centre of each cake with a teaspoon or so of the blackcurrant filling.

7. Make the icing at the last minute. Break the dark chocolate into pieces and melt it slowly in a bowl over a pan of simmering water. Once melted, whisk in the caster sugar until it has dissolved into the warm chocolate. Add the soured cream and whisk – it should be creamy and luscious. Leave it to cool down slightly, as it will thicken and be easier to spread.

8. Spread the icing on top of the cakes, placing the cut-out pairs of fairy wings in the centre. Decorate with some dark chocolate buttons and a sprinkle of red edible glitter for that extra touch of wickedness.

T I P

Remember not to add too much sugar to your blackcurrant filling. It should remain a little bit tart, as this will balance out the sweetness of the sponge cake and the dark chocolate icing.

Prince Charming's Kisses

I know this might come as a bit of a shock, but the real Prince Charming is less of a charmer than his name would suggest. I'm sorry to say it, but he's a self-obsessed pretty boy whose only goal in life is to prance around on horseback saying smarmy things to young princesses and nothing much else. I mean, have you ever seen Prince Charming do anything practical; has he put up a shelf, done the vacuuming, made dinner or put the bins out? No, of course not – he's all show and no substance! Or do you think I am being too cruel? Perhaps I am. Well, one good thing I can say about him is that he did show me how to make some delicious homemade chocolates that he'd once made reluctantly for a friend's birthday. I grimace when I say this, but yes, they are actually a little bit charming . . .

MAKES 24 CHOCOLATES
100g desiccated coconut
250g plain chocolate
25g unsalted butter
6 chocolate cupcakes (I make a batch of Bad Fairy Cakes (page 40), minus the filling and icing, and use half of them for this recipe)
1½–2 tablespoons Amaretto (you could also use rum or coffee liqueur if you prefer)

1. Line a large baking sheet with clingfilm and set to one side. Place the desiccated coconut on a small plate.

2. Break the chocolate into pieces and melt slowly with the butter in a bowl over a pan of simmering water. Once melted, let the chocolate cool slightly for a few minutes.

3. Take your cooled chocolate cupcake sponges and put them into a mixing bowl. Break them up with a fork so that they turn to crumbs. Add the Amaretto or your spirit of choice to the cake crumbs and mix well. Taste at this stage to make sure you're happy with the flavour. You can of course omit the alcohol completely if you prefer.

4. Next, add 2 tablespoons of the melted chocolate to the cake crumb mixture and stir well – the mixture should now be sticking together.

TIP

I often make these chocolates to give away as presents, and this is a great way to get kids involved with cooking. They look adorable popped into mini-cupcake cases and placed in a gift box.

5. Take about a teaspoon of the mixture and, using your hands, roll it into a little ball and pop it on a plate or tray. Repeat this process until all the mixture is used up – you should get 24 chocolates out of this amount of mixture.

6. Now you need to coat the chocolates. Place each ball of mixture in the rest of the melted chocolate, making sure it is well covered, then remove and roll it in the coconut to get a nice coating. If you aren't keen on coconut, these taste equally as good with just the simple chocolate coating. Once covered, place on the lined baking tray. Repeat this process until all the chocolates are covered, then put them into the fridge for 1–2 hours, until they have firmed up.

7. Store in the fridge in an airtight container and bring them out about 10 minutes before you want to eat them.

A
Royal
AFFAIR

Princess and the Pea Soup

The Good King's Casserole

The Castle's Chocolate-Spice Cupcakes

Snow Queen Cookies

'After chatting to the Snow Queen I realised she isn't as frosty as she first appears; perhaps making cookies has thawed her icy heart?'

Princess and the Pea Soup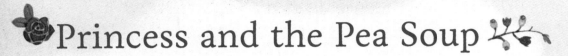

It is said that only a true princess is sensitive enough to feel a pea nestled under twenty mattresses and twenty feather beds. This may well be true, but I am confident that we non-royals will easily find the pea in this dish! For those of us who happen to be stranded outside a prince's castle on a wet and stormy Friday night, this delicious soup is warming, moreish and comforting. And if your prince has a penchant for alfresco, this soup can also be served chilled on a hot summer's day.

MAKES 2 HEARTY BOWLS
OR 4 DAINTY FAIRY CUPS
400ml water
400g frozen peas (or fresh
   if you prefer – adjust the
   cooking time accordingly)
10g butter
2 jumbo salad onions or 4–5
   spring onions, finely chopped
fresh mint leaves (finely chop
   approx. 2 tablespoons and
   keep 1 whole leaf per bowl/
   cup for decoration)
2 tablespoons double cream
salt and ground white pepper
pea shoots and
   sweet-pea flowers,
   to decorate (optional)

1. Bring the water to the boil, then add the peas and cook until tender. This should take about 7 minutes.

2. While the peas are cooking, melt the butter in another pan and add the finely chopped salad onions. Fry the onions over a medium/low heat so that they soften but don't colour – this should take about 3–4 minutes.

3. When the peas are cooked, don't drain them. Remove about half a tablespoon from the pan and put them to one side to use for decoration later.

4. Place the cooked peas, cooking water, onions and chopped mint into a blender or food processor and blitz until smooth. Add the double cream and give it a final blitz, then season with salt and pepper.

5. To serve (either hot or chilled in bowls or teacups), place a single pea at the bottom of the dish and pour the soup on top. On top of the soup place a single mint leaf with a couple of peas on top so that it resembles a split pea-pod. Alternatively, if you are using fresh peas you could decorate the soup with fresh pea shoots or, if you can source them, some sweet-pea flowers, it's entirely up to you.

The Good King's Casserole

I couldn't quite contain my excitement when I met the King of Fairytale Land, although I can't really remember what happened, to be honest. I just did the same thing we all do when we meet or see someone important or famous – I stood, frozen to the spot, with a rather gormless look on my face. Oh well. Despite my lacking the ability to string a comprehensible sentence together, the King was extremely courteous and kindly told his cook to give me the recipe for his favourite meal; this royally good chicken casserole. It really is fit for a king!

THIS RECIPE WILL
COMFORTABLY SERVE
2 PEOPLE, POSSIBLY 3,
DEPENDING ON THE SIZE OF
YOUR CHICKEN BREASTS!

2 large whole chicken breasts
  (on or off the bone is fine,
  preferably with skin on)
salt and freshly ground
  black pepper
1 tablespoon olive oil,
  plus a small knob of butter
  for frying
1 large onion, roughly chopped
1 garlic clove, crushed
150g chestnut mushrooms,
  cut into quarters
500g potatoes, peeled and cut
  into large chunks
2–3 carrots, peeled and cut
  into large chunks
100g fresh or frozen peas
1½ tablespoons
  mushroom ketchup
½ teaspoon dried rosemary
2 bay leaves
200ml white wine
500ml chicken stock

1. Season the chicken breasts with salt and pepper.

2. In a large pan or a casserole dish that can be used on the hob, heat the oil and butter and fry the chicken breasts for a few minutes on a high heat until they are nicely browned. Remove from the pan on to a plate and place to one side.

3. Turn the heat down, then add the onion and garlic to the pan and fry for a couple of minutes until softened. Add the mushrooms, potatoes, carrots, peas and mushroom ketchup, give everything a good stir and season with a decent dosing of salt and pepper. Add the rosemary and bay leaves and cook for a few minutes.

4. Return the chicken to the pan, then add the white wine and the chicken stock. Turn the heat up and bring to the boil, then turn the heat down low, pop a lid on and leave the casserole to simmer on the hob for 1½–2 hours, until the chicken and vegetables have cooked through and the sauce has reduced.

5. Serve in large bowls, with a hunk of bread on the side to mop up the gravy!

The Castle's Chocolate-Spice Cupcakes

I have always dreamed of living in a fairytale castle; the ultimate being the castle belonging to the King of Fairytale Land, which is to die for – it has its own indoor heated pool and a walled grass tennis court! I don't know about you, but I quite fancy having my own private turret to potter around in. Sadly my mortgage won't stretch that far, so I will have to make do with the odd picnic in the glorious castle grounds. I should say that the King's castle does have a rather excellent tea shop, but it can be quite pricey and exclusive for us common folk; so having embarked upon a bit of undercover café reconnaissance, here is the recipe for the castle's speciality cupcakes. These chocolate cupcakes are laced with heady cardamom and topped with a delicious ginger buttercream icing. All pinched by yours truly for our picnic hampers – yum!

MAKES 12

Cake batter

110g softened unsalted butter
110g caster sugar
2 large eggs
110g self-raising flour
2 tablespoons cocoa powder
1 teaspoon baking powder
1½ teaspoons ground ginger
4 cardamom pods, seeds
   removed and ground to
   a powder in a pestle
   and mortar
2 tablespoons milk

1. Preheat the oven to 190°C/170°C fan/gas mark 5 and fill a 12-hole muffin tray with paper muffin cases.

2. Cream the butter and caster sugar together until pale and fluffy, then add the eggs one at a time, mixing well.

3. Sift the flour, cocoa powder, baking powder, ground ginger and cardamom and add to the mixture a third at a time along with the milk, mixing well to ensure that all the dry and wet ingredients are combined.

4. Spoon the mixture into the prepared muffin tray, filling the paper cases about two-thirds full. Place in the centre of the oven and bake for about 20 minutes, until the tops are springy to touch, or a skewer comes out clean. Leave the cakes to cool on a wire rack.

Icing
60g softened unsalted butter
250g icing sugar, sifted
1 teaspoon ground ginger
2 tablespoons milk

To decorate
gold edible glitter (optional)
edible star confetti (optional)

5. While the cakes are cooling, make the ginger buttercream icing. Place the softened butter in a large bowl and whip it up using an electric hand mixer. Add the icing sugar a bit at a time and cream it with the butter. Next add the milk and the ground ginger and mix well until you are left with a smooth, thick, creamy icing.

6. Once the cakes have cooled completely, pipe or spread the icing on top and decorate – I like to add a dusting of gold edible glitter and some edible star confetti to the tops of my cakes to make them look truly regal!

The Castle Tea Shop Lunch Menu

❧ *SOUPS* ❧

Grandiose Gazpacho

Princely Potato and Leek

Queen's Carrot and Coriander

❧ *THE CASTLE'S CLUB SANDWICHES* ❧

Regally Rare Roast Beef

Coronation Chicken

Majestic Melted Mozzarella

❧ *AFTERS* ❧

The Castle's Chocolate-Spice Cupcakes

Jubilee Jelly and Ice Cream

Splendid Scones with Jam and Clotted Cream

Snow Queen Cookies

I quite like the idea of being an ice maiden for a day, don't you? I sometimes think we warm, friendly and cuddly types could benefit from being a bit glacial – it's always the slightly frosty ones who are deemed alluring and mysterious. So I was quite surprised to hear that the Snow Queen herself has got a bit bored of being so icy all the time. She has given up her day job of piercing people's hearts with sadness and has set up an ice sculpture business instead. And when she's not chiselling away at a block of ice, she spends her time in her ice palace baking tasty treats in an attempt to thaw her frozen fingers. These scrumptious almond and coconut cookies are one of her specialities; they really do warm the heart.

MAKES 12

50g softened unsalted butter,
  plus extra for greasing
50g golden caster sugar
1 large egg, beaten
1 teaspoon almond essence
85g plain flour
25g ground almonds
50g desiccated coconut, plus
  a little extra for sprinkling
1 teaspoon baking powder

1. Preheat the oven to 190°C/170°C fan/gas mark 5. Lightly grease and flour 2 large non-stick baking sheets.

2. Cream the butter and sugar together in a large bowl until pale and fluffy, then stir in the beaten egg and the almond essence.

3. Add the flour, ground almonds, coconut and baking powder and stir well until they are all fully incorporated.

4. Take a couple of teaspoons of the mixture, roll it in your hands to form a little ball, and place it on one of the prepared baking sheets. Sprinkle with a little more desiccated coconut. Repeat this process until all the mixture is used up.

5. Place the trays in the oven and bake the cookies for about 10–12 minutes, until they are golden brown and just firm to the touch – you don't want them to be rock hard but neither do you want a liquid gooey centre.

6. Remove from the oven and leave to cool thoroughly before serving. These are superb with a good cup of coffee – enjoy!

BELLE
AND
her
BEAU

Beauty and the Beast Burgers

Pretty Sweet Potatoes

Devoted Dips

True Love's Hearts

'Talk about feeling
like a spare part;
these two are
adorable but a bit
lovey-dovey for
my liking.'

Beauty and the Beast Burgers

I have a lot of respect for Beauty; not only is she gorgeous, intelligent, generous and extremely loving towards the poor tormented Beast, but she is a huge fan of burgers – who would have thought it? It's so refreshing to meet a young woman these days who isn't completely obsessed with her waistline. I'm not saying for one minute that we should forget about eating healthy stuff, but there are times when we need a little comfort food in our lives, and a decent homemade burger never did anyone any harm. Here are both Beauty and the Beast's favourite burger recipes; be prepared to fall hopelessly in love with them.

 ## Beauty's Plucky Chicken Burgers

MAKES 4

2 large skinless chicken breasts
salt and freshly ground
   black pepper
6 tablespoons buttermilk
100g fresh breadcrumbs
   (just blitz some white bread
   in a food processor)
1 teaspoon paprika
1 teaspoon dried chilli flakes
   (optional)
100g plain flour, seasoned
   with salt and pepper
1 large egg, beaten
4 or 5 tablespoons olive oil,
   enough for shallow frying

1. Take your chicken breasts and slice them both in half through the middle so that you are left with 4 escalopes. Depending on the size of your chicken breasts you should get 4 medium-sized burgers from this amount of chicken, but you can adjust the amount to suit you.

2. Place the chicken pieces in a large bowl, season well with salt and pepper, and spoon over the buttermilk. Make sure all the chicken is well coated in the buttermilk and then pop it into the fridge for a few hours to marinate – this will ensure that the chicken stays lovely and tender when cooked.

3. Preheat the oven to 200°C/180°C fan/gas mark 6. Put the breadcrumbs into a dish and add the paprika, chilli flakes (you can leave these out if you can't stand the heat) and some salt and pepper. Stir well. Put the seasoned flour and beaten egg in their own separate dishes.

4. Take a piece of chicken and dip it into the flour, covering it well. Then dip it into the beaten egg and finally into the breadcrumbs. Make sure it's well coated, then place to one side on a plate while you prepare the remaining pieces.

5. Line a large baking tray with foil and grease lightly with olive oil. Heat the oil in a large frying pan on a high heat, getting it really hot. You can test whether it's hot enough by dropping a breadcrumb into it – if it starts to fry you're there! Fry the chicken in the hot oil one piece at a time so that they are nicely browned – this will only take about a minute per burger. Place the fried chicken on the prepared baking tray and finish off in the oven for about 10–15 minutes, until they are cooked through.

6. Serve in a large bread roll with plenty of mayonnaise, crispy lettuce and tomato – beautiful!

Beast's Best Beef Burgers

MAKES 4

1 medium white onion
2 tablespoons olive oil,
  for frying
salt and freshly ground
  black pepper
450g braising steak
2 teaspoons of
  Worcestershire sauce

1. Peel the onion, then put it into a food processor and blitz until very finely chopped.

2. Heat 1 teaspoon of the oil in a small pan and fry the onion, with a pinch of salt, on a medium heat until it's softened.

3. Dice the beef and trim off any large lumps of excess fat. Place in the food processor with the cooked onion, the Worcestershire sauce and plenty of salt and pepper, and blitz until the meat is finely ground.

4. Shape the ground beef mixture into burger patties – you can probably get about 4 medium-large burgers from this mixture.

5. Line a large plate with some clingfilm. Put the burgers on the plate and pop into the fridge for a good couple of hours so that they can firm up. Bring them out of the fridge about 15 minutes before you want to cook them so that they warm up a little.

6. You can pop these burgers under a hot grill for about 15 minutes, or fry them in a large frying pan in some olive oil for the same amount of time – I find you get more flavour into the burger by frying them.

7. I like to serve them in large bread rolls with lots of ketchup, a little Dijon mustard, some lettuce, tomato, onion and some sliced gherkin – scrummy!

Pretty Sweet Potatoes

We all love and, let's face it, need a good chip, don't we? Whether fat or thin, wedged, skinny or curly, you can't beat them. I adore using good old baking potatoes to make my chips, but these sweet potato wedges are great when you fancy something a little different. Pretty sweet indeed!

SERVES 4

2–3 tablespoons olive oil
4 large sweet potatoes
salt and freshly ground
  black pepper

1. Preheat the oven to 220°C/200°C fan/gas mark 7. Line a couple of large baking trays with baking foil and lightly grease the foil with a little of the olive oil.

2. Peel and wash your sweet potatoes, then cut them into nice chunky-chip sized wedges.

3. Tumble the chips on to the prepared baking trays and drizzle the remaining olive oil over them. Sprinkle with salt and a little pepper, then, using your hands, make sure all the chips have been oiled and seasoned.

4. Place in the oven and cook for about 30–40 minutes, until they are just starting to caramelise around the edges.

5. These chips are the perfect accompaniment to my Beauty and the Beast Burgers, but they are just as good piled high with some Devoted Dips on the side.

Devoted Dips

It's nice to be loyal and committed to someone or something in life, isn't it; whether it's your family, your friends, your pets or the gym. Of course I am dedicated to all (but one) on that list, but I am also a proud and unashamed devotee of food and a definite disciple of these delicious dips.

Faithful Blue Cheese

 This deliciously creamy and cooling blue cheese dip is wonderfully simple to make.

SERVES 4

100g Roquefort cheese
(you could also use Stilton
or Gorgonzola)
5 tablespoons low-fat
mayonnaise
3 tablespoons lemon juice

1. Place the Roquefort in a small bowl and mash it up using the back of a fork.
2. Add the mayonnaise and lemon juice and stir well.
3. This dip is fabulous with most things barbecued and is the perfect dip for all your crudités.

Beloved Barbecue Sauce

 I adore a good, spicy homemade barbecue sauce; and this recipe is so tasty and easy to make, you won't want to dip your chips in anything else!

SERVES 4

6 tablespoons tomato ketchup
2 teaspoons
Worcestershire sauce
2 tablespoons light soy sauce
1½–2 teaspoons
cayenne pepper
1 teaspoon paprika

1. Place all the ingredients except for the cayenne pepper in a small serving bowl and mix well.
2. Stir in 1 teaspoon of the cayenne and have a taste – if you want it spicier, add more to suit you.

 Doting Garlic and Chive Mayo

You really can't beat freshly made mayonnaise, and this garlic and chive version is a little stunner. I often make this as an accompaniment for a grilled chicken salad or lamb koftas in pitta bread – delish!

MAKES ENOUGH FOR 4

1 large egg yolk
1 teaspoon English mustard
150ml olive oil
1 teaspoon white wine vinegar
2 garlic cloves, crushed
a bunch of fresh chives about
   the width of your finger,
   finely chopped
salt and freshly ground
   black pepper

1. Put the egg yolk, mustard and 1 teaspoon of the olive oil into a food processor (or bowl if you are using a hand mixer) and blitz for about 30 seconds.

2. Leave the blade running and very slowly add the rest of the olive oil in a steady, thin, trickle. If you add the oil too quickly the mixture won't thicken and you'll end up with a runny mess, so do go slow!

3. Once all the olive oil has been poured in, add the vinegar and stop mixing.

4. Spoon the mayonnaise into a bowl, add the crushed garlic and chopped chives and season with salt and pepper.

5. The mayonnaise will keep quite happily in the fridge for a couple of days as long as it's in an airtight container.

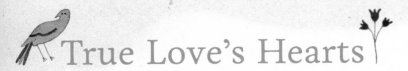

True Love's Hearts

Because I'm a soppy romantic at heart, I have always believed in true love. I know lots of people don't and that's fine, we're all entitled to our own opinion. For me it's the feeling of all-consuming excitement, slight bewilderment and nervous anxiety that tells me that I am unmistakably in love. Or maybe that's the champagne cocktails talking . . . Anyway, whether you're a passionate, starry-eyed idealist like me or a level-headed cynic, I'm sure you'll fall head over heels with these lovable, rose-scented biscuits. Adore them!

MAKES 12

Biscuit dough
50g softened unsalted
   butter, plus a little extra
   for greasing
50g caster sugar
1 large egg, beaten
150g plain flour
25g ground almonds
½ teaspoon rosewater

Icing
100g icing sugar, sifted
4 teaspoons milk
a couple of drops of rosewater
a tiny dash of pink food
   colouring paste

To decorate
edible glitter (optional)

1. In a large bowl, cream together the butter and sugar until pale and fluffy. Add the egg and mix well.

2. Next, stir in the flour, ground almonds and rosewater and bring the mixture together to form a ball of dough, using your hands. If the mixture is a little sticky, simply add a little more flour.

3. Place the biscuit dough in a polythene bag and put it into the fridge for about 30 minutes to firm up.

4. Preheat the oven to 210°C/190°C fan/gas mark 6½ and grease 2 large baking sheets with a little butter.

5. When the dough is ready, roll it out on a lightly floured work surface to about 3mm thick. Using a cutter (I use a heart-shaped one which measures about 6cm, with it being romantic and all that), cut out the biscuits, placing them on the prepared baking sheets as you go, and remembering to leave a gap of about 5cm between them. You should be able to get about 12 biscuits out of this mixture if you are using a cookie cutter of this sort of size.

6. Place in the oven for 5–10 minutes, until the biscuits are just starting to turn golden.

7. Once cooked, remove from the oven and place on a wire rack to cool completely before icing.

8. When the biscuits have cooled, make the icing. Sift the icing sugar into a bowl and add the milk teaspoon by teaspoon, along with a couple of drops of rosewater, stirring well until you have a smooth icing. You want it to be thin enough to drizzle over the biscuits but thick enough to set. Add the pink food colouring paste to the icing and mix well.

9. Pipe or drizzle the pretty pink icing on to each biscuit, with a sprinkle of edible glitter to make them look truly gorgeous. Leave the icing to set, then store in an airtight container.

FAIRY FOLK

Enchanted Forest Gateau

Fairy Chocolate Cups

Goblin Granitas

'Took a nice long walk in the Enchanted Forest today; a couple of the goblins were up to no good but after a stern look they scuttled off.'

Enchanted Forest Gateau

The Enchanted Forest is a melting pot of all things magical; it is full of supernatural forces, mystical beings and dangerous creatures. You'll find trees laden with magic lanterns, toadstool rings littering the forest floor and purple smoke rising slowly from the chimney of a nearby witch's cottage. All sounds quite idyllic, doesn't it? But, however tranquil it might seem, the forest isn't a place to walk through alone at night, and many who have gone for a post-dinner stroll have never returned. Though for daytime ramblers like me, the forest is perfectly safe and is a great source for gathering wild and magical ingredients for my pantry. It was after a spot of enchanted fruit picking that I came up with the idea for this gateau; a magical twist on the classic recipe from the neighbouring Black Forest. This enchanted version will leave you spellbound!

SERVES 10–12

Cake batter

220g softened unsalted butter,
  plus extra for greasing
220g caster sugar
4 large eggs
200g self-raising flour
40g cocoa powder
1 teaspoon baking powder

Filling

750g fresh cherries
  (you need 500g once you've
  pitted them)
2½ tablespoons kirsch
3 tablespoons Bonne Maman
  Berries and Cherries
  Conserve (you can get this
  in most supermarkets, but
  if you can't find it, a good
  cherry conserve will do)
300ml double cream
1 tablespoon caster sugar

1. Preheat the oven to 190°C/170°C fan/gas mark 5. Grease and flour a round 23cm spring-form cake tin, 7cm deep, with a little unsalted butter.

2. To make the sponge, first cream the butter and caster sugar together until pale and fluffy, then add the eggs one at a time, mixing well.

3. Sift the flour, cocoa powder and baking powder into a bowl and add to the mixture a third at a time, mixing well to ensure that all the dry and wet ingredients are combined.

4. Spoon the mixture into the prepared cake tin and level the top. Place in the centre of the oven and bake for about 35–40 minutes, until the top is springy to touch, or a skewer comes out clean. Leave the cake to cool in the tin for about 15 minutes before removing the outer ring of the case and leaving it to cool down completely.

5. While the sponge is cooling you can get on with making the cherry filling. Pit the cherries (I find the easiest way of doing this is to simply cut round the stone) and place them in a non-stick pan with the kirsch and the jam. Cook on a medium to low heat for about an hour, until the fruit is tender, the juices have reduced down and you are left with a deliciously soft, sticky compote. Remove from the heat and leave to one side to cool down.

Topping
100g plain chocolate
  (make sure you get one
  which is 70% cocoa solids)
1 teaspoon kirsch

To decorate
sugar flowers (optional)
white edible glitter (optional)

6. Next, place the double cream and the caster sugar into a bowl and whisk until the cream thickens and forms soft peaks – it should hold its shape and be of a spreadable consistency. Pop it into the fridge until you are ready to fill the cake.

7. To make the topping, break the dark chocolate into pieces and melt it slowly in a bowl over a pan of simmering water. Once melted, let the chocolate cool slightly for a few minutes and then add the kirsch. Leave to cool.

8. When the cake is cold, take a large serrated bread knife and gently slice it in half horizontally. Because I use a spring-form cake tin with a base I leave the lower tier of the cake on the base as this makes it much easier to serve!

9. Spread the whipped cream over the bottom half of the cake and gently spoon the cherry compote on top of the cream. Place the other half of the cake on top and sandwich together.

10. Finally, spread the cooled melted chocolate over the top of the cake and decorate as desired. I prefer to keep it simple, and I top the gateau with a simple sugar flower and a sprinkling of white edible glitter.

11. Because of the fresh cream, this cake is best served on the day it's made, but it will keep until the next day if you store it in the fridge.

Fairy Chocolate Cups

Fairies, like us humans, have the potential to be two-faced; on the outside they are incredibly delicate, beautiful, kind and cheeky, but on the inside some can be ugly, evil, malicious little beings. Despite some bad experiences with the odd fairy's wicked side, I'm lucky that most of my fairy friends are truly lovely and have been generous enough to give me the recipe for this magical chocolate dessert – a real taste of fairyland.

**MAKES 4 RAMEKINS OR
LITTLE TEACUPS**

200g good-quality
  milk chocolate
150g good-quality
  dark chocolate
150ml double cream
1 tablespoon dark rum
a handful of pistachio nuts
edible glitter (optional)

1. First break the milk and dark chocolate into pieces and melt slowly in a bowl over a pan of simmering water.

2. Once melted, pour the chocolate into a non-stick pan and add the double cream and the rum. Gently heat the mixture on the hob over a medium-low heat until it is smooth and slightly thickened. Remove from the heat and set to one side to cool for a few minutes.

3. While the chocolate and cream mixture is cooling, shell and chop the pistachio nuts. Next, heat up your frying pan and dry toast the nuts, which should literally take just a minute or two – you just want to colour them slightly.

4. Sprinkle some of the nuts into the base of your ramekins or teacups, and pour the chocolate mixture on top. You can sprinkle more nuts on top if you have any going spare.

*'I met a lady in the meads,
Full beautiful – a faery's
child, Her hair was long,
her foot was light,
And her eyes were wild.'*

5. Cover loosely with clingfilm and put the chocolate cups into the fridge for an hour or so to set.

6. Bring them out of the fridge about half an hour before you want to eat them so they aren't stone cold, and sprinkle a little edible glitter on top for a dash of fairy magic.

7. These little pots of chocolate luxury are best served either as they are or with some amoretti biscuits or biscotti on the side for dipping!

Goblin Granitas

When it comes to goblins I don't have a lot of patience – would you? They are the most irritating creatures and I urge you, if you ever have the misfortune to run into a gaggle of the mischievous little critters, to turn and run. If they latch on to you, you've had it – they will follow you home and will be inside messing the place up before you've closed the door. I happened to meet a couple of very cheeky goblins who are perfectly amenable but only if I'm stern with them; if I let my guard down they'd be scuttling around my pantry in no time. We met at a party that some of my fairy friends had thrown, and I have to give it to them, they know how to make a good drink. These tangy, bright green apple granitas are their favourite tipple.

MAKES 1

ice cubes: about a handful
    per person
Sourz Apple Liqueur or Bison
    Grass Vodka: a 25ml shot of
    spirit per glass
apple juice, freshly pressed,
    not from concentrate:
    a 25ml shot per glass
green food colouring:
    1 drop per glass
cocktail umbrellas

1. Place the ice cubes in a food processor and blitz until they are crushed into a snowy powder.

2. Spoon some of the crushed ice into a small tumbler.

3. Pour over the apple liqueur or vodka and the apple juice, then add the food colouring and give it a stir.

4. That's it; add a cocktail umbrella and drink!

TIP

These granitas are great for parties, especially Hallowe'en – they are such a violently vivid shade of green they look fabulously evil. If you want to make a child-friendly version, simply leave out the alcohol.

Off to
NEVERLAND

Peter Pancakes

Captain Hook's Fish Pie

Jolly Roger Jelly

Tinkerbell's Trifle

'I have a slight rum-headache as I write this morning; there was a piratical knees-up, need I say more?'

Peter Pancakes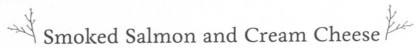

Peter Pan is the boy who never grew up; everything he does is an adventure, and to top it off he can fly! He's met mermaids, Indians, fought pirates and causes no end of mischief with Tinkerbell. And if all this youthful exuberance and courageousness wasn't enough, Peter is also pretty adventurous in the kitchen, cooking up all the Lost Boys' favourite dishes. His famous savoury stuffed pancakes are a delight, and although they won't make you live for ever, they might make you feel a tiny bit younger at heart.

Smoked Salmon and Cream Cheese

SERVES 2–4

100g smoked salmon,
  torn into strips
150g low-fat cream cheese
juice of ½ a lemon
a bunch of fresh chives about
  the width of your finger,
  finely chopped
4 plain pancakes
  (homemade or shop-bought)
50ml double cream
salt and freshly ground
  black pepper
lemon wedges, to serve

1. Preheat the grill until it's very hot, and lightly grease an ovenproof dish approximately 30 x 21 x 6cm.

2. Put the smoked salmon strips and cream cheese into a bowl and mix well. Add the lemon juice and chives and stir until everything is well combined.

3. Lay one of the pancakes flat on a chopping board or plate and spoon a quarter of the mixture horizontally along the middle. Roll the pancake up loosely and place in the prepared baking dish. Repeat this process for the other 3 pancakes and add them to the dish.

4. Drizzle over the double cream, lightly season with salt and pepper and place under the grill for about 10–15 minutes, until golden brown.

5. Serve with a green salad and wedges of lemon.

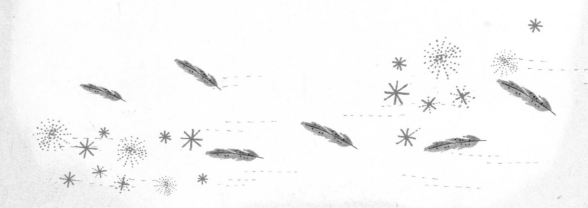

Bacon and Mushroom

SERVES 2–4

1 teaspoon olive oil
120g (approx. 4 rashers)
   smoked back bacon,
   rind removed, cut into
   small pieces
1 small onion, finely chopped
150g chestnut mushrooms,
   finely chopped
salt and freshly ground
   black pepper
4 plain pancakes
   (homemade or shop-bought)
100ml double cream
30g Cheddar cheese, grated

1. Preheat the grill until it's very hot, and lightly grease an ovenproof dish approximately 30 x 21 x 6cm.

2. Heat the olive oil in a non-stick pan and fry the bacon for 5 minutes or so, until it starts to colour.

3. Add the onion and fry until it starts to soften, then add the mushrooms and season well with salt and pepper. Cook for a further 5–10 minutes, until the mushrooms have cooked down and any liquid has cooked out.

4. Lay one of the pancakes flat on a chopping board or plate and spoon a quarter of the mixture horizontally along the middle. Roll the pancake up loosely and place in the prepared baking dish. Repeat this process for the other 3 pancakes and add them to the dish.

5. Drizzle over the double cream and scatter the grated Cheddar on top. Place under the grill for about 10–15 minutes, until golden brown.

6. Serve with a mixed salad.

Spinach and Ricotta

SERVES 2–4

10g butter
200g baby spinach
salt and freshly ground
 black pepper
20g pine nuts
250g ricotta cheese
4 plain pancakes
 (homemade or shop-bought)
50ml double cream
20g Parmesan cheese, grated

TIP

I've suggested that you can use shop-bought pancakes for these recipes as, let's face it, we don't always have the time to stand there flipping homemade ones; however, if you do have a spare moment it's well worth the effort, and it's something the kids will love to get involved with.

1. Preheat the grill until it's very hot, and lightly grease an ovenproof dish approximately 30 x 21 x 6cm.

2. Melt the butter in a non-stick pan over a medium heat, then add the spinach and let it wilt down. Season with plenty of salt and pepper.

3. Once the spinach has cooked down, place it in a fine sieve and drain off the excess liquid.

4. Return the spinach to the pan, add the pine nuts and gently warm through. Take the pan off the heat and mix in the ricotta, stirring everything really well. Season with plenty of salt and pepper.

5. Lay one of the pancakes flat on a chopping board or plate and spoon a quarter of the mixture horizontally along the middle. Roll the pancake up loosely and place in the prepared baking dish. Repeat this process for the other 3 pancakes and add them to the dish.

6. Drizzle over the double cream and sprinkle over the Parmesan. Place under the grill for about 10 minutes, until golden brown.

7. Serve with a mixed salad.

HAVE YOU SEEN THIS PIRATE?

ONE-PATCH FLINT
WANTED FOR SMUGGLING A PORTION OF THE CAPTAIN'S FISH PIE

REWARD
5,000 GOLD COINS

Captain Hook's Fish Pie

Now this might make you shiver in your timbers, but I'm rather a fan of Captain Hook. I know he's missing a right hand, his beard is too long and there's that peculiar ticking crocodile following him around, but he is one of the only pirates I've met that has good manners. He never once tried to make me walk the plank! I spent a very pleasant evening with the Cap'n aboard his jolly ship, and he treated me to a superb fish pie supper with a rather large rum and coke to wash it down with. All that's left to say, my cockles, is yarrr!

SERVES 2

500g haddock fillets
500ml whole milk
1 bay leaf
salt and ground white pepper
25g butter
1 tablespoon plain flour
75g Cheddar cheese, grated
a handful of fresh curly parsley,
   finely chopped

Topping
750g potatoes,
   peeled and chopped
50g salted butter
50ml milk

1. Place the haddock fillets skin side down in a large frying pan and cover with the milk. Add the bay leaf and season well with salt and pepper. Place the pan over a medium heat and poach the fish in the milk for about 7–10 minutes, until cooked – the milk should gently simmer but not boil.

2. When the fish is cooked, remove it from the poaching liquid and place it on a chopping board. Remove the skin and any bones and flake the fish into chunks. Place in an ovenproof dish, approximately 30 x 21 x 6cm.

3. Pass the hot poaching liquid through a sieve into a jug and put to one side.

4. Melt the butter in a non-stick pan over a medium heat and add the flour, stirring to make a roux. Add the fish poaching liquid to the roux a little at a time, stirring continuously as you go, until you have a smooth sauce with the consistency of double cream. Add the grated cheese to the sauce, followed by the chopped parsley, then stir well and season with salt and pepper. Pour the sauce over the flaked haddock and mix well. Leave the filling to cool down a little.

5. While the filling is cooling, preheat the oven to 220°C/200°C fan/gas mark 7 and make the mashed potato for the topping. Bring a large pan of salted water to the boil, add the potatoes and cook for about 20–25 minutes, until completely cooked through. Drain, then mash the potatoes with the milk, butter, salt and ground white pepper until smooth and creamy.

6. Spoon or pipe the mashed potato on top of the pie filling. Place the pie dish on a baking tray (to catch any spills!) and cook in the oven for about 25 minutes, until golden brown and piping hot all the way through.

7. I like to serve this pie simply with some peas and a nice juicy wedge of lemon to squeeze on top – lovely stuff!

Jolly Roger Jelly

Ahoy! Like the rather lovable pirate rogues on board the Jolly Roger, I love a good party, and no party is complete in my eyes without pudding. So, if you're after a good old-fashioned swashbuckling dessert, this delightful sweetie-filled jelly is for you. Packed with plenty of pieces o' eight, it will satisfy even the smallest shipmates in your crew. Enjoy, me hearty!

MAKES ENOUGH JELLY FOR
A 570ML JELLY MOULD
SERVES 4
5 sheets of fine leaf gelatine
400ml smooth orange juice
   (make sure it is not
   from concentrate)
170ml water
1–2 tablespoons caster sugar
a handful of chopped fresh
   strawberries or clementine
   segments, or some
   jelly sweets
edible glitter, preferably
   silver or gold

1. Soak the gelatine leaves in a bowl of cold water for about 5 minutes, or according to the instructions on the packet. If you are making one large jelly you will need 5 leaves of gelatine to set it, but if you are making smaller jellies 4 leaves should be enough.

2. While the gelatine is soaking, pour the orange juice and water into a pan and add the caster sugar a dessertspoon at a time, tasting as you go – I find 2 tablespoons is enough for me, as I like a zingy jelly, but you might prefer it sweeter. Bring the mixture to a gentle simmer but don't let it boil.

3. Remove the gelatine leaves from the water, shake off any excess liquid and add them to the hot orange juice. Leave to simmer gently for a couple of minutes, stirring occasionally. Remember not to let the juice boil, as that can affect the set of the jelly. Take the mixture off the heat, pour into a jug and leave to cool down.

4. Take a handful of fruit or sweets and place them in the bottom of your jelly mould(s) – scatter them around a bit and sprinkle in a small dusting of edible glitter. Gently pour in the cooled jelly mixture and place in the fridge for 3–4 hours, until the jelly has set.

5. Remove from the mould(s) just before you are ready to devour it. You should see the fruit or sweeties clustered at the top of the jelly like little jewels. I recommend serving this wonderfully wobbly creation either on its own or with a large scoop of vanilla ice cream – yum!

Tinkerbell's Trifle

It's commonly known that dear little Tinkerbell once had a reputation for being a bit cantankerous. Always whizzing around, her tiny wings flapping in a furious frenzy; she really was a fuming fairy. But just like the best of us, her frantic displays of crossness were caused by one thing: too much to drink. Poor Tink had been terribly envious of Wendy, but instead of handling her jealousy by going for a long walk, having a nice bubble bath or sipping a steaming hot cup of fairy-tea, she took to the pirates' ship, with a thimble in her tiny hand, and filled it to the brim with grog. Of course, due to her petite stature, intoxication occurred quite quickly and she was soon overcome by feelings of joy, sadness, guilt and, of course, extreme rage. It took the Lost Boys a good couple of days and lots of strong coffee to bring her back to normal, I can tell you! Nowadays the little lightweight stays well clear of the strong stuff, although she still likes to add a slosh of her favourite tipple to her terrific trifle. It's just a thimbleful (or two), I promise!

SERVES 6–8

Base

120g trifle sponge fingers
100ml sherry or liqueur,
  e.g. Tia Maria

Fruit filling

1 x 290g tin of blackcurrants
  in juice, drained
350g fresh strawberries,
  stalks removed, halved
1 tablespoon caster sugar
2 tablespoons cold water
1 tablespoon dark rum

Custard

100ml whole milk
200ml double cream
1 teaspoon vanilla extract
3 large egg yolks
25g caster sugar
1½ teaspoon cornflour

1. Place the sponge fingers in the base of a large glass bowl, to make a nice layer – you might need to break some up a bit, or put them on their sides; it doesn't have to be neat.

2. Pour the sherry or your chosen liqueur over the sponges and leave to one side to soak in.

3. Next, make the fruit filling. Put the blackcurrants and strawberries into a medium pan, then add the caster sugar and water and cook on a medium-low heat for about 5–10 minutes, until the fruit starts to soften. When it's ready, spoon the fruit mixture on top of the trifle sponges. Sprinkle over the rum. Leave to one side to cool thoroughly.

4. While the fruit is cooling, make your custard. Put the milk, double cream and vanilla extract into a non-stick pan and place over a medium heat until it's hot but not simmering.

Topping
300ml double cream
6–8 strawberries, sliced

10g plain chocolate, grated,
   for sprinkling

TIP

If you'd rather not make
a boozy trifle, you can omit
the alcohol and simply soak the
sponges in fruit juice instead.
I sometimes use the juice that the
blackcurrants come in and just
add a little sugar and water to it.

5. Blend the egg yolks, caster sugar and cornflour together in
   a bowl, and when the vanilla cream is hot, slowly add it
   to the egg mixture little by little, making sure you stir it
   gently as you go. When all the cream is mixed into the eggs,
   return the mixture to the pan and cook on the lowest possible
   heat, stirring gently until the custard thickens. Make sure the
   heat is very low and that you stir constantly, otherwise the
   custard will split. When it's thickened, remove from the heat
   and leave to cool for about 5–10 minutes before pouring it
   over the top of the now cooled fruit.

6. Next, whisk the double cream for your topping so that it
   forms soft peaks, using a hand or electric whisk. Spoon the
   cream on top of the custard layer and decorate with fresh
   sliced strawberries and the grated chocolate. Cover loosely
   with clingfilm and pop into the fridge to firm up for about
   3 hours or so before serving.

I'll Huff
AND
I'll Puff

Three Little Pigs in Blankets

Huff 'n' Puff Pork

Piggy No.1's Apple Sauce

The Wolf's Sticky Ribs

'The little pigs had been very busy; one had built a new house out of bricks which was very fancy.'

Three Little Pigs in Blankets

Pigs are known to be incredibly intelligent creatures, smarter than the average Border Collie, it's often said; so it came as little surprise to me when I heard that the Three Little Pigs were rather into interior design. Piggy No. 1 had a thing for the outdoors and liked bringing natural materials into the home. Piggy No. 2 was similarly taken by the lure of natural design but preferred a slightly bolder, minimalist look. Finally, Piggy No. 3 was very much a creature who liked his comforts, well, don't we all . . . he liked to use modern materials in his house and couldn't resist luscious colourful fabrics and textiles. In particular he was a huge fan of big, soft, cosy blankets and liked nothing better than wrapping himself up in fleecy comfort, perhaps having a nice nap on the sofa at the same time. When the other piggies came round for tea on a cold and windy afternoon, they took instantly to the warm, fluffy blankets, and so the word spread – pigs in blankets became all the rage, and to this day you will rarely find a little pig without one, especially at birthday parties or Christmas . . .

MAKES 6 'THREE PIGS IN BLANKETS' OR 18 'SINGLE PIGS IN BLANKETS'

9 rashers of smoked streaky bacon (½ a rasher per sausage)

18 pork chipolatas

1 teaspoon olive oil, for frying

1 small onion, finely chopped

3 slices of thick white bread, crusts removed, cut into chunks

8 fresh sage leaves

salt and freshly ground black pepper

500g ready-rolled puff pastry

1 large egg, beaten

1. Preheat the oven to 220°C/200°C fan/gas mark 7, and lightly grease a large baking tray with a little olive oil.

2. Cut the bacon rashers in half, removing any thick rind, then wrap a piece around each sausage and place them on the prepared baking tray. Now, I prick my sausages, I always have and I always will – I can't help it, but if you prefer not to that's up to you. Put them into the oven for about 30 minutes, until they are cooked through and golden brown. Remove from the oven and leave to one side to cool down slightly. Leave the oven on.

3. Next, make the stuffing. Heat the oil in a small non-stick pan and fry the finely chopped onion for about 5 minutes, until soft but not browned. Place the fried onion in a food processor along with the chunks of bread, the sage leaves and a liberal seasoning of salt and pepper. Blitz until all the ingredients are well blended together.

4. Lightly grease a second large non-stick baking tray with a little olive oil. Roll out your pastry and divide it into 6 equal squares (or 18 squares if you are making single pigs in blankets). Lay 3 of the bacon-wrapped sausages side by side on each pastry square, making sure that they are placed so that you can fold the pastry over them to form a rectangular shape. Spread a couple of teaspoons of the stuffing over the sausages, brush the joining edges of the pastry with beaten egg and seal the parcels up. Place on the prepared baking tray, brush with more beaten egg, and bake in the oven for 20–30 minutes, until the pastry is cooked and they are golden brown.

5. The larger, pasty-sized piggies are delicious served hot from the oven with a dollop of mashed potato and some peas, but they are also fantastic served cold in any pastry-lover's lunchbox. The single pigs are a perfect party nibble and make a great bite-sized treat for a picnic.

Huff 'n' Puff Pork

It's no wonder that two of the little pigs met rather a sticky end. They built lovely, cosy little homes, but they weren't any match for the wolf and his mighty cyclonic breath; with just one puff, their houses tumbled to the ground and they soon found themselves on the menu. Just like all of us can be from time to time, the wolf was a little indecisive and couldn't decide on how to cook his porky prizes. But after some thought, Piggy No. 1 soon became slow roasted, tender pulled pork, piled high inside a large buttered bread roll with a dollop of homemade apple sauce and a dash of cider vinegar. There are worse ways to end up I suppose . . .

SERVES 6

2kg boneless shoulder of pork
salt and freshly ground
  black pepper
3 bay leaves

1. Preheat your oven to its highest temperature.

2. Using a sharp knife, score the fat on top of your pork shoulder. Rub plenty of salt into the skin and into the scores you've made, and also season the underside of the pork with salt and pepper. Leave the joint to stand for about 5 minutes and you'll see that quite a lot of moisture will come out of the fat. Dab the pork dry with some kitchen paper and then re-salt; this will help you get really crisp crackling. Place the pork in a large roasting tray, skin side up, with the bay leaves scattered around, and roast for 30 minutes, until you see the skin start to puff up and crackle.

3. Remove the roasting tray from the oven and cover the pork with a double layer of tin foil. Return it to the oven and reduce the temperature to 170°C/150°C fan/gas mark 3½. Cook for 3½ –4 hours, until the meat is tender and falling apart. Leave it to rest for about 10 minutes before shredding it with a fork.

4. You could serve this with all the usual roast dinner trimmings, but it is delicious stuffed inside a crusty bread roll with a little splash of cider vinegar and a spoonful of Piggy No. 1's Apple Sauce. And if you are fortunate enough to have any pork left over, please don't throw it away or give it to the dog; it is absolutely delicious cooked up with some onions, garlic, red or green peppers, tomatoes and a splash of balsamic vinegar and stirred through some steaming hot pasta. Yum, yum, yum!

Piggy No.1's Apple Sauce

100g large Bramley cooking
  apples (approx. 2)
1 teaspoon caster sugar,
  plus more if needed
1 tablespoon water
10g unsalted butter

1. Peel and chop the apples and put them into a small non-stick pan with the sugar and water. Cook on a low heat for about 10–15 minutes, until the apples have become mushy. Taste at this stage to see if you want to add any more sugar – I like my apple sauce quite tart, but you may want it sweeter.

2. When the apples are cooked, take them off the heat and stir in the butter.

3. Leave to cool completely before serving.

'Little pig, little pig,
let me come in.'
'No, no, not by the hair
on my chinny chin chin.'
'Then I'll huff,
and I'll puff,
and I'll blow your
house in.'

The Wolf's Sticky Ribs

*After all that huffing and puffing, the Big Bad Wolf was in need of a breather and a good
dinner; it's hard work blowing down two houses in one day, you know! And what could be
better than enjoying a relaxing evening in the garden, taking in the warm summer's air while
various slabs of delicious juicy meat smoke away on the barbecue. These scrumptiously tender
pork ribs are marinated for twenty-four hours in a sticky, spicy sauce, to tenderise them and
give them oodles of flavour. You can pop them on the barbecue, or slow cook them in the oven
if rain clouds should appear.*

MAKES ENOUGH RIBS FOR
2—3 PEOPLE

4 tablespoons tomato ketchup
2 tablespoons dark soy sauce
½ tablespoon
    Worcestershire sauce
1 tablespoon runny honey
2 garlic cloves, crushed
½ teaspoon dried chilli flakes
1 teaspoon cayenne pepper
1 teaspoon paprika
salt and freshly ground
    black pepper
3 half-racks of pork ribs

1. In a small bowl, mix up the marinade: tomato ketchup,
    soy sauce, Worcestershire sauce, honey, garlic, spices, salt
    and pepper.

2. Place the pork ribs in a large dish and smother them in the
    marinade, making sure they are well covered. Cover the dish
    and leave in the fridge to marinate for 24 hours.

3. When you're ready to cook your ribs, put them into
    a large roasting tray lined with tin foil. Preheat the oven to
    240°C/220°C fan/gas mark 9 and cook the ribs for 15 minutes.
    Then turn the heat right down to 140°C/120°C fan/gas mark 1
    and cook them for a further 2½–3 hours, until they are charred
    on the outside and meltingly tender on the inside.

4. If I'm barbecuing these I find it easier to wrap them in foil and
    place them on a slightly cooler part of the barbecue for about
    an hour or so before removing the foil and finishing them off
    over the flames. The slower you cook them the more succulent
    they will be.

5. Serve straight up, with some buttered corn on the cob and
    plenty of napkins to wipe those sticky fingers!

UNDER
the
SEA

The Sea Witch's Scallops

Little Mermaid Crab Cakes

Landlubber's Lemon Cheesecake

Pebble Beach Bars

'I went to the beach today with the Little Mermaid. She's a complete flirt; flaunting those new legs of hers at any man who walked by.'

The Sea Witch's Scallops

I was rather impressed when I first met the Sea Witch; she is very much a woman of high status within her watery realm. Like the best of us she can be a bit temperamental on occasions; she might conjure up the odd whirlpool or strong north-easterly wind to mess with a few sailors, but she's not half as wicked as many of the land-based witches can be. I happen to that think she's rather misunderstood; plus, she knows a good thing or two about seafood. I assure you, scallops done the Sea Witch way are divine; you'll be diving in for more!

SERVES 2 AS A STARTER,
WITH 3 SCALLOPS PER
SERVING, BUT YOU CAN
ADJUST THE QUANTITIES
AS YOU LIKE

1 bag of rocket leaves (you need
    about a handful per serving)
5 rashers of smoked streaky
    bacon, rind removed, cut into
    small pieces
12 walnut halves
1 tablespoon olive oil,
    for frying
6 scallops (3 per person)
juice of ½ a lemon
salt and freshly ground
    black pepper
lemon wedges, to serve

1. Place a handful or so of rocket on your serving plates.
2. Fry the bacon in a non-stick pan until crispy – don't add any oil, as the bacon will fry in its own fat. When it's almost cooked, toss in the walnuts just to give them a light toasting. Scatter the bacon and walnuts among the rocket leaves.
3. Heat the olive oil in a large frying pan on a medium to high heat, and when it's hot pop in the scallops. Pan fry them for about a minute on each side, and just before they are done, squeeze over the lemon juice. Place the scallops on top of the salad and season to taste – I find that a little pepper is all it needs.
4. Serve with a wedge of lemon on the side and a hunk of crusty bread!

Little Mermaid Crab Cakes

I spent a nice relaxing day at the beach with the Little Mermaid, who is completely lovely, but sadly mute because of that daft trade-in she did with the Sea Witch to get herself a pair of legs. Don't get me wrong, I'm not knocking her legs – she has the perfect pins – and by heck does she enjoy flashing them about! But a lady's life shouldn't just be about showing her bits off to sailors, should it? Of course, I have to admit I was green with envy. Put it this way; I don't suffer from cankles, but I probably wouldn't blow over in a force nine gale! Anyway, fortunately for me and all of us slightly sturdy people out there, these tasty crab cakes are both healthy and full of flavour, so they shouldn't add any inches to your ankles – phew, what a relief!

MAKES 8

100g fresh breadcrumbs
  (I just blitz up some white
  bread in a food processor)
5 spring onions
1 red chilli, seeded
a handful of fresh coriander
350g crab meat (approx. 3
  dressed crabs – I use both the
  brown and the white meat)
zest and juice of 1 lime
½ teaspoon ground coriander
2 teaspoons fish sauce
1 large egg, beaten
salt and freshly ground
  black pepper
3 tablespoons olive oil,
  plus a little for greasing

1. Place your breadcrumbs in a large bowl.

2. Put the spring onions, red chilli and fresh coriander into a food processor and blitz until they are all finely chopped together. Add to the breadcrumbs and stir well.

3. Add the crab meat to the breadcrumb mixture along with the lime zest and juice, the ground coriander, fish sauce and egg and mix well. Taste the mixture and season with a little salt and pepper if you need to.

4. Cover the bowl with clingfilm and place in the fridge for about 30 minutes to chill before you start cooking.

5. Preheat the oven to 200°C/180°C fan/gas mark 6. Lightly grease a large baking tray with a little olive oil and set to one side.

TIP

If you'd rather make lots of little crab cakes you can get about 16–20 smaller patties out of this amount of mixture. Cook them using the same method, but reduce the cooking times: fry the cakes for about 30 seconds, then give them up to 5 minutes in the oven, keeping an eye on them to make sure they don't overcook and burn.

6. Put the olive oil into a large frying pan over a fairly high heat. Take a few spoonfuls of the crab mixture and, using your hands, form a patty (about the size of your palm). Place it in the hot oil and fry for 1 minute on each side, then put it on the prepared baking tray while you repeat the process with the rest of the mixture. You should have enough mixture to make about 8 medium-large crab cakes.

7. When all the crab cakes are sealed and on the baking tray, place them in the oven and bake for about 5–10 minutes, to ensure they are cooked through.

8. Remove from the oven and squeeze some fresh lime juice over the top of the crab cakes.

9. I like to serve these little beauties with a simple salad or some new potatoes. A little Tabasco or some sweet chilli sauce also works well on the side.

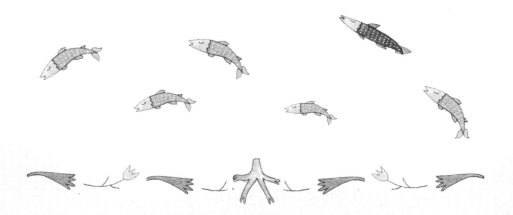

Landlubber's Lemon Cheesecake

It has been three long, blissful, well-grounded, non-nauseous years since I have been on a boat. The last time, and I hope it will be the last time, that I took a journey by boat around the shores of Fairytale Land, I really did feel like I was about to die! All you habitual cruisers and yacht dwellers no doubt think I am exaggerating to the point of no return, which is fine; I can take stick for being utterly useless on the sea, because it's true! In the past I tried various magical potions in an attempt to suppress my landlubber's instinct, but this time I stumbled on an alternative solution. To my surprise, and despite the horrendous lurching of the boat in question, I found myself feeling a bit peckish, so I sought solace in something sweet – a slice of tangy lemon cheesecake. Now, I wouldn't say the cheesecake cured me but I definitely felt less sickly; so the next time I dare board a boat, my pockets will be full of this luscious, lemon cheesecake: the landlubber's lifesaver!

SERVES 8–10

150g digestive biscuits
100g plain chocolate
50g unsalted butter
750g mascarpone
30g icing sugar
50ml double cream
zest of 2 lemons
juice of 2–2½ lemons

1. Grease a 23cm spring-form round cake tin with some butter and line the base of the tin with baking parchment.

2. Crush your digestive biscuits; you can do this by simply blitzing them quickly in a food processor. Alternatively, use them as a way of releasing some stress – place them in a sealable, strong plastic bag and bash away with a rolling pin until you are left with a fine crumbly mixture.

3. Put 75g of the chocolate and all the butter into a small pan and melt together over a low heat. Remove from the heat and stir in the crushed biscuits, making sure they are all well covered in the chocolate. Pour the biscuit mixture into the prepared tin, spread out over the base and press down firmly, using your fingers or the back of a spoon so that you have an even base. Place in the fridge to set for 15 minutes or so while you make the filling.

4. Place the mascarpone, icing sugar and double cream in a large bowl and give it a quick whisk.

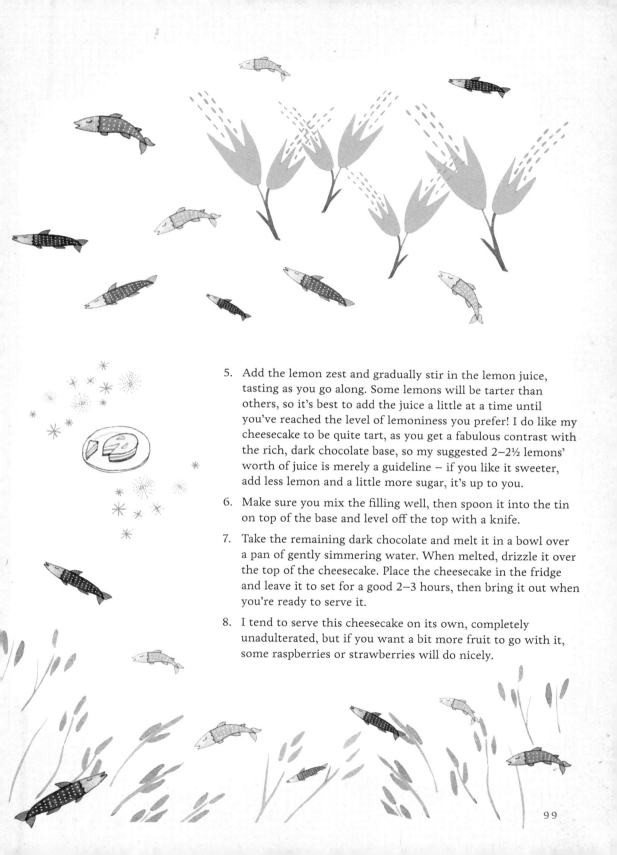

5. Add the lemon zest and gradually stir in the lemon juice, tasting as you go along. Some lemons will be tarter than others, so it's best to add the juice a little at a time until you've reached the level of lemoniness you prefer! I do like my cheesecake to be quite tart, as you get a fabulous contrast with the rich, dark chocolate base, so my suggested 2–2½ lemons' worth of juice is merely a guideline – if you like it sweeter, add less lemon and a little more sugar, it's up to you.

6. Make sure you mix the filling well, then spoon it into the tin on top of the base and level off the top with a knife.

7. Take the remaining dark chocolate and melt it in a bowl over a pan of gently simmering water. When melted, drizzle it over the top of the cheesecake. Place the cheesecake in the fridge and leave it to set for a good 2–3 hours, then bring it out when you're ready to serve it.

8. I tend to serve this cheesecake on its own, completely unadulterated, but if you want a bit more fruit to go with it, some raspberries or strawberries will do nicely.

Pebble Beach Bars

Personally I've always preferred a nice pebbly beach to the white sandy type filled to the brim with sun-worshippers. You can have so much more fun finding pretty shells, interesting rocks, and of course spend hours scouring sparkling rock pools for interesting little critters, just like I did on a day out with the Little Mermaid. At about 3.30 p.m. that afternoon, having put in hours of strenuous rock-pooling, we needed a sugary snack, and these little pebbly bars of biscuity, chocolaty, nutty, marshmallowy goodness were the result – they are the ultimate sweet 'n' salty treat.

MAKES ABOUT 20 BARS

100g unsalted butter, plus
  a little extra for greasing
300g plain chocolate
150g rich tea biscuits
150g digestive biscuits
3 Crunchie bars
100g salted peanuts
100g mini-marshmallows

1. Grease a disposable foil roasting tray (about 29.8 x 23.5 x 3.8cm) with a little unsalted butter.

2. Put the butter and chocolate into a non-stick pan and melt together over a low heat.

3. In a large bowl, bash up the biscuits and the Crunchie bars – you don't want to turn them to dust, but you want a nice rubble-like texture. Mix in the peanuts and marshmallows.

4. Pour over the melted butter and chocolate mixture and mix well so that all the dry ingredients are well coated in the chocolate. It will look like there's not enough chocolate, but trust me, there will be.

5. Tip the mixture into your prepared foil tray and press down firmly.

6. Cover with clingfilm and place in the fridge to set for a few hours. Once set, cut into bars and store in an airtight container.

YOU
Shall
GO
TO THE
BALL

Cinderella's Pumpkin Pie

Good Fairy Cakes

Ugly Sister Sundae

'Had dinner with
Cinders who was
showing off her new slippers –
they were glass and gorgeous.'

Cinderella's Pumpkin Pie

There are some days – and I think we all have them – when I feel a bit like Cinderella; and I don't mean the glamorous, Doris-Day-do'd version she's now become. I'm talking about the soot-stained, broken-nailed one with a torn apron! But between you and me, I think Cinders has been overdoing it with the shopping recently. Since becoming a fairytale princess, Cinders now frequents the finer shoe boutiques of Fairytale Land (rather than tending to her pumpkin patch) on a daily basis; honestly, that prince won't know what's hit his wallet! But I shouldn't moan about her really. Cinders worked hard for her success amid all the bullying and teasing from her unsightly stepsisters, and I have to respect her for that. So, in celebration of Cinderella's humble beginnings, here is my recipe for the perfect pumpkin pie; it's sweet, aromatic and a whole lot cheaper than a pair of glass slippers!

SERVES 8

Base

200g plain flour
a pinch of salt
50g icing sugar
100g cold butter
approx. 2 tablespoons
   cold water

Filling

1 medium butternut squash
   (or you could use a small
   culinary pumpkin)
1 teaspoon cinnamon
½ teaspoon ginger
½ teaspoon ground nutmeg
1 teaspoon mixed spice
½ teaspoon salt
1 teaspoon vanilla extract
2 large eggs, beaten
200g soft brown sugar
100ml evaporated milk

1. Cut the squash or pumpkin into large pieces and scrape out the seeds and fibres. Put the pieces of squash or pumpkin into a roasting dish, skin side up, and bake for about 30–40 minutes, until tender. Leave to cool, then scoop out the flesh from the skins and blitz it in a food processor until puréed. Place the purée in a fine sieve and leave to drain for a couple of hours.

2. If you're making your own pastry case you can do that while the purée is draining. Place the flour, salt, icing sugar and butter in a large bowl and rub the butter into the flour to form a crumbly mixture.

3. Add the water a spoonful at a time – you may need more or less water than I've suggested here, so just add it gradually until you can bring the dough together with your hands.

4. Bring the dough together into a ball, wrap it in clingfilm or place it in a polythene bag, and put it into the fridge for about 30 minutes to firm up.

5. Preheat the oven to 210°C/190°C fan/gas mark 6½ and lightly grease a 23cm flan dish with a little butter. Roll out the pastry to line your dish and blind bake it in the oven for about 20 minutes, until it is golden brown. Once cooked, leave it to cool down. Reduce the oven temperature to 200°C/180°C fan/gas mark 6.

6. Place the drained pumpkin purée in a large bowl. Add the spices, salt and vanilla extract. In a separate bowl, beat the eggs with the sugar and add this to the purée, stirring well.

Topping
200ml double cream
1 tablespoon dark rum
½ tablespoon maple syrup
a sprinkling of ground
   cinnamon

TIP
I know that this recipe
requires quite a bit of time in
the kitchen, but one way you
can save a moment or two is
by using a pre-made sweet
shortcrust pastry case.

7. Slowly pour in the evaporated milk and mix well so that you have a smooth and silky mixture. Pour this into the cooled pastry case and bake in the oven for about 30–40 minutes, until the filling has set – it should still have a slight wobble in the middle. Leave the pie to cool completely.

8. When the pie has cooled, put the double cream and rum into a large bowl and whisk until it forms soft peaks. Spread on top of the pie.

9. Finally, drizzle the maple syrup on top and sprinkle with a tiny bit of cinnamon. Leave in the fridge to chill for about an hour before serving, then get stuck in!

SLIPPER SALE!

THIS SATURDAY AT MIDNIGHT

SHOPPERS WILL RECEIVE
A COMPLIMENTARY SLICE OF
PUMPKIN PIE ON ARRIVAL

PLEASE CONTACT CINDERELLA
FOR MORE INFORMATION

Good Fairy Cakes

I sometimes fantasise about being the Good Fairy. Wouldn't it be lovely to get all those boring tasks done with the simple swish of a wand: the washing, the dusting, the ironing . . . oh well, we can dream. The Good Fairy is generous, sweet, lovely and beautiful, and these scrumptious cupcakes are made in her honour, albeit without a wand! Now, go and be a goody-two-shoes and get baking!

MAKES 12

Cake batter
110g softened unsalted butter
110g caster sugar
2 large eggs
110g self-raising flour
1 teaspoon baking powder
2 tablespoons milk
½ teaspoon almond essence

Filling
½ a 312g jar of good
   shop-bought lemon curd

Icing
60g softened unsalted butter
250g icing sugar, sifted
1 tablespoon milk
½ teaspoon almond essence

To decorate
silver dragees (optional)
edible glitter (optional)

1. Preheat the oven to 190°C/170°C fan/gas mark 5 and fill a 12-hole muffin tray with paper muffin cases.

2. Cream the butter and caster sugar together until pale and fluffy, then add the eggs one at a time, mixing well.

3. Sift the flour and baking powder and add to the mixture a third at a time, along with the milk and almond essence, mixing well to ensure that all the dry and wet ingredients are combined.

4. Spoon the mixture into the prepared muffin tray, filling the paper cases about two-thirds full. Place in the centre of the oven and bake for about 20 minutes, until the cakes are pale gold in colour and springy to touch, or a skewer comes out clean. Leave them to cool on a wire rack.

5. While the cakes are cooling, you can make the icing. Place the softened butter in a large bowl and whip it up, using an electric hand mixer. Add the icing sugar a bit at a time and cream it with the butter. Next add the milk and the almond essence and mix well until you are left with a smooth, thick creamy icing.

6. Once the cakes are cooled, angle a small sharp knife and cut a round out of the middle of each cake, leaving a hole in the centre. Cut the rounds in half (to make fairy wings) and set aside. Fill the centre of each cake with a teaspoon or two of lemon curd, then either spread or pipe the icing on top, placing a pair of the cut-out fairy wings in the centre.

7. For a final flourish of fairy sparkle, add a few silver dragees and a sprinkling of edible glitter to each cake.

Ugly Sister Sundae

I was slightly anxious about meeting this pair for lunch. Their reputation is fairly awful, it has to be said, and like we all do, I find it incredibly cringeworthy when I have to meet people that I know I won't like. So I wouldn't say I enjoyed my time with the ugly sisters; they are repulsive to look at, they talk complete rubbish and they are incredibly vain (goodness knows why!). But it wasn't the worst lunch I've had, and that's probably because the dessert was absolutely superb. The sisters are undoubtedly selfish, horrid and rather ineffective creatures, but by heck can they make a delicious sundae. Packed with ice cream, nuts, bananas, chocolate sponge, fresh whipped cream and butterscotch sauce, this really is a fabulous dessert – and it's definitely not ugly!

MAKES 4

4 chocolate cupcakes, cut into
  chunks (I make a batch of
  Bad Fairy Cakes (see page
  40), minus the filling and
  icing, and use 4 of them for
  this recipe)
a handful of whole
  blanched almonds
300ml double cream
2 large bananas
vanilla ice cream
  (approx. 2 scoops per sundae)
a jar of Opies maraschino
  cocktail cherries

1. If you are making your own chocolate cupcakes, make a batch following the recipe on page 40 and leave them to cool completely. You'll need 4 of them – cut them into chunks.

2. To make the butterscotch sauce, put the butter and light brown sugar into a non-stick pan over a medium heat and bring to the boil. Don't stir the mixture, just swirl it gently around the pan from time to time. Leave the mixture to bubble steadily for about 5 minutes, then take the pan off the heat and slowly stir in the double cream. Turn the heat down, then return the pan to the heat briefly, just to make sure the cream is thoroughly mixed in, and you are left with a smooth butterscotch sauce. Pour the sauce into a jug and leave to one side.

3. Next, place a small non-stick frying pan on the heat and pop in the almonds. Let them toast gently for about 3–5 minutes, until they are just starting to turn golden brown, then put them into a mortar and give them a quick bash up with the pestle – you want them to remain quite chunky, so don't crush them completely. If you don't have a pestle and mortar you can chop them up a bit using a sharp knife.

I adore a good old-fashioned ice cream sundae. They look fabulously retro on the dinner table, kids love them and you can have lots of fun inventing your own flavour combinations. Fresh raspberries or strawberries are a great substitute if you don't fancy using bananas, and instead of butterscotch sauce you could make a homemade chocolate sauce just by melting together some plain chocolate, double cream and a little butter.

Butterscotch sauce
50g unsalted butter
100g light brown muscovado
   sugar
100ml double cream

4. Pour the double cream into a medium-sized bowl and whisk it up, using an electric or hand whisk, until it forms soft peaks but is stiff enough to pipe. Spoon into your piping bag (I use disposable ones for this sort of thing and just snip the end off).

5. Peel the bananas and cut into small chunks. Get the ice cream out of the freezer to soften up a little before you start to construct your sundae. Get ready 4 tall ice cream sundae glasses or long cocktail glasses.

6. I always have to have a cocktail cherry at the bottom of my sundae, so I drop a couple into the bottom of each sundae glass. Put a layer of chocolate sponge on top, then banana, ice cream, whipped cream, a few nuts and a spoonful or two of the butterscotch sauce, and repeat the process until you reach the top of the glass. Top off the sundae with some whipped cream, a sprinkle of almonds, a final drizzle of butterscotch sauce and, of course, a cherry on top.

7. Finally, grab a long-handled spoon and get stuck in!

A HOUSE MADE FROM *bread* AND *cakes...*

Hansel and Gretel's House Gingerbread

Breadcrumb and Butter Pudding

Witch Pops

'I helped Hansel scatter a trail of breadcrumbs in the afternoon; he's still so worried about getting lost.'

Hansel and Gretel's House Gingerbread

We can't help but feel for Hansel and Gretel, the poor little mites. Thrown out of home by their wicked and conniving stepmother, they were left to fend for themselves in the dark wild forest, where they discovered an amazing gingerbread house and almost met their maker at the hands of a gruesome, cannibalistic old witch. Quite enough drama for two little children to contend with, I'd say! But despite their terrifying experience, they lived to tell the tale and bought back some of the witch's delicious cakes, one of which was her gingerbread; proper old-fashioned, stick-to-your-ribs gingerbread – perfect for fattening up the children . . .

SERVES 12

200g treacle
50g unsalted butter
50g soft dark brown sugar
75ml milk
300g self-raising flour, sifted
2 teaspoons mixed spice
3 teaspoons ground ginger
½ teaspoon grated nutmeg
½ teaspoon baking powder
1 large egg, beaten

1. Preheat the oven to 200°C/180°C fan/gas mark 6 and grease a 1kg loaf tin with butter.

2. Put the treacle, butter, sugar and milk into a non-stick pan over a medium heat until thoroughly melted together. Remove from the heat and set to one side.

3. Sift the flour into a large mixing bowl and stir in the mixed spice, ginger, nutmeg and baking powder.

4. Pour in the liquid ingredients, then add the egg and mix well.

5. Spoon the mixture into your prepared loaf tin and bake for about 40 minutes, until the gingerbread is springy to touch and a skewer comes out clean.

6. Turn the cake out on to a wire rack and leave to cool completely. Once cool, wrap it well in tinfoil to store – this cake keeps really well and it will gradually become stickier as the days go by. It makes a delicious afternoon treat served plain or spread with a little butter. It's also very tasty roughly crumbled over vanilla ice cream.

Breadcrumb and Butter Pudding

Since his rather harrowing experience of being dumped in the forest by his evil stepmother and almost getting eaten by a witch, Hansel has become a little paranoid. To this day, if he's out and about, he cannot help but scatter a trail of breadcrumbs behind him so that he can find his way home. Honestly, has the boy never heard of GPS? Needless to say, due to his breadcrumb-scattering habit, Hansel has rather a large stash of lovely crusty bread in his pantry, and I can think of no better way to use it than in a sumptuous bread pudding. Gloriously creamy, with vanilla, rum and spices, this really is a pudding to come home to.

SERVES 4

300ml double cream
300ml whole milk
1 vanilla pod, seeds scraped out
3 large eggs and 1 large
   egg yolk
100g golden caster sugar
125g sultanas
1 tablespoon navy rum
200g crusty white farmhouse
   bread, buttered on both sides
   and cut into triangles
½ teaspoon ground cinnamon
½ teaspoon grated nutmeg

1. Pour the double cream and milk into a pan, then add the vanilla seeds and bring to the boil.

2. Crack the 3 whole eggs into a large bowl, add the extra yolk, and beat gently. Stir in the caster sugar, then gradually add the hot cream/milk, stirring as you go to make a thin custard. Pour the custard through a fine sieve into a large jug.

3. Place the sultanas in a small bowl with the rum and leave them to soak.

4. Lightly butter a deep ovenproof dish (approximately 30 x 21 x 6cm) and layer in the buttered bread triangles, sprinkling in the rum-soaked sultanas and the rum as you go. Pour over the custard mixture and push the bread into it so that each piece is well soaked and covered. Sprinkle on the cinnamon and nutmeg and leave to sit for about 20 minutes.

5. Preheat the oven to 180°C/160°C fan/gas mark 4. Place your pudding dish in an oven tray and pour some boiling water into the tray so that it comes just halfway up the sides of the dish. Bake in the oven for 40–50 minutes, until the top of the pudding is golden and the custard is set.

6. Leave to cool slightly before serving (if you can wait – I often can't!) and enjoy with a slosh of single cream or even a drizzle of melted chocolate. Mmmm!

WITCH'S BREW

10 sun-dried bat wings
3 organic newt eyes
5 pairs of pre-waxed spiders' legs
1 sparrow's foot
1 litre of slug juice – without bits
1 teaspoon sugar – to taste

Place all the ingredients in
a medium-sized cauldron and
bring to a steady bubble.
Simmer for 1 hour. Leave to
cool, then serve on ice.

Witch Pops

The witch whom Hansel and Gretel happened to run into is one of the most frightening witches in all of Fairytale Land; she really is a horror. For starters, she's downright sneaky. Building her cottage out of gingerbread and sweeties to lure innocent, unsuspecting little children into her rotten lair is just so, so creepy. Secondly, and most disturbingly, she fattens up the little darlings she catches, cooks them and eats them for dinner! Now of course none of us would ever condone this terrible cannibalistic behaviour, but we should be open-minded and appreciate that some of the dishes the witch cooked to capture her 'prey' are actually pretty good. One of my favourites is this recipe idea for fresh fruit-juice ice lollies with little jelly sweets frozen inside. You can experiment with different fruit juices, soft drinks, different sweets or even fresh fruit to suit you. They are incredibly easy and fun to make and are a healthy summer treat for little children and adults alike.

MAKES 12–16 LOLLIES
DEPENDING ON THE SIZE OF
THE MOULD YOU USE, REFER
TO 'ENCHANTED ESSENTIALS'
FOR FURTHER DETAILS

ice lolly moulds
   (and lolly sticks if needed)
1 litre of fruit juice of your
   choice (I use different
   ones: pineapple, orange,
   pomegranate, apple)
jelly sweets or fruit

1. Place a few jelly sweets or pieces of fruit inside each lolly mould.

2. Top up each mould with fruit juice. Add sticks if using.

3. Pop into the freezer.

4. Once frozen, remove the lollies from the moulds and enjoy!

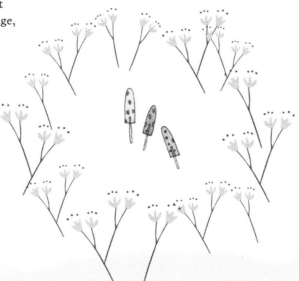

THE
better
TO
eat
YOU
with

Woodcutter's Wild Mushroom Soup

Granny's Cottage Pie

Red Riding Hood's Basket

Big Bad's Simple Vanilla Cakes

'I saw the big bad wolf running away from Granny's cottage; I was rather concerned, he was wearing a bonnet.'

Woodcutter's Wild Mushroom Soup

Is it just me, or do most maidens these days have a bit of a thing for woodcutters? Maybe it is just me, but I think there's something rather appealing about a man who can handle an axe and also be at one with his native woodland surroundings. Little Red Riding Hood was extremely lucky that her local hunky woodsman was around to save the day when she waltzed straight into the jaws of the Big Bad Wolf. It was undoubtedly a heroic rescue by our man in a checked shirt, so to celebrate his terrific axe-wielding efforts, I've included this recipe for his favourite soup; it's healthy, hearty and wholesome – just like he is. Swoon!

SERVES 4

25g butter

½ tablespoon olive oil

1 medium onion, roughly chopped

500g mushrooms, finely sliced (use a mixture if you like – I like using chestnut or field mushrooms)

salt and freshly ground black pepper

1 tablespoon mushroom ketchup

600ml vegetable stock

1 tablespoon double cream

1. Heat the butter and oil in a large pan and fry the onion for a few minutes until it softens.

2. Add the mushrooms and fry for about 5 minutes. Add a little salt and pepper at this point, along with the mushroom ketchup. The mushrooms will shrink down and will start to release their liquid.

3. Once the mushrooms are cooked through, add the stock and simmer for about 5 minutes.

4. Remove from the heat and blend the mixture (in batches if necessary) in a food processor or blender until smooth.

5. Return the soup to the pan over a low heat and stir in the double cream. Season with salt and pepper.

6. Serve with hunks of crusty bread.

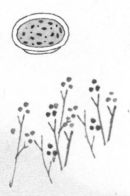

'Oh Grandmother, what big ears you've got,' she said.

'The better to hear with, my dear.'

'Grandmother, what big eyes you've got.'

'The better to see with, my dear.'

'What big hands you've got, Grandmother.'

'The better to catch hold of you with, my dear.'

'But, Grandmother, what big teeth you've got.'

'The better to eat you up with, my dear.'

Granny's Cottage Pie

I adore my granny; she's kind-hearted, generous and likes nothing more than curling up in her chair with a crossword and a decent drop of Scotch. Sadly, my granny isn't a natural born cook; she once complained about a chicken she was roasting, saying, 'There's not much meat on this bird' – she happened to be cooking it upside down! Red Riding Hood's granny, however, is a dab hand in the kitchen, and one of her favourite family dishes (and mine for that matter) is a good old-fashioned cottage pie. If you're after a simple, delicious and comforting family supper, this is the recipe for you. I recommend serving it with some pickled red cabbage on the side.

SERVES 4

Filling

½ tablespoon olive oil,
  for frying
500g minced beef
1 large white onion, peeled
  and finely chopped
2–3 large carrots, peeled
  and finely chopped
4 tablespoons peas
  (frozen are fine to use
  if you don't have fresh)
½ tablespoon
  mushroom ketchup
½ tablespoon
  Worcestershire sauce
1 bay leaf
a handful of fresh flat-leaf
  parsley, roughly chopped
salt and freshly ground
  black pepper
300ml beef stock
  (a stock cube is fine
  if you don't have fresh)

1. Preheat the oven to 210°C/190°C fan/gas mark 6½.

2. Heat the olive oil in a large pan, then add the minced beef. When the mince is browned, remove it from the pan and set to one side. Try to keep as much of the meat juice in the pan as possible.

3. Turn the heat down to medium, add the onions and carrots, and fry for about 5 minutes, until they start to soften.

4. Return the minced beef to the pan, add the peas, mushroom ketchup, Worcestershire sauce, bay leaf and parsley, and season with salt and pepper. Add the stock, cover the pan and leave to simmer on a low heat for about 30–40 minutes, until the vegetables are cooked through and the filling has reduced and thickened up a little.

Topping
750g potatoes, peeled and
  quartered
50g salted butter
50ml milk
salt and ground white pepper

TIP

I often make the filling for the
cottage pie the day before I'm
going to use it and just leave it in
the fridge ready to be topped with
mash and baked. If you want to be
extra naughty with your topping,
you could sprinkle some grated
Cheddar cheese over the mashed
potato before baking.

5. While the filling is cooking you can prepare the topping.
    Boil the potatoes in water until soft, then drain them and
    mash them with the butter, milk, salt and pepper.

6. When the filling is cooked, spoon it into an ovenproof dish.
    Top with the mashed potato and bake in the oven for about
    30 minutes, until golden brown.

Red Riding Hood's Basket

*I've always felt that Little Red Riding Hood's blatant stinginess was the cause of her downfall.
She skips merrily through the forest and all she has in her basket is a measly piece of cake and
some butter? The Big Bad Wolf must have rubbed his paws with glee when he saw her coming;
he was looking forward to a nice bit of ham, a couple of boiled eggs, maybe some cheese,
some crisps even, but there were no such goodies. So what is a hungry wolf supposed to do?
We can't blame him for gobbling up Red and her granny – if she'd just put some proper treats
in her basket his tummy would have been full and no one would have been eaten. So may
this be a lesson to us all; when filling your baskets, fill them well. You can practise by making
this delicious meringue basket brimming with luscious chocolate cream and forest fruits.
But remember, don't scrimp, or the wolf will get you!*

SERVES 6–8

Meringue

2 teaspoons cornflour
2 teaspoons white
 wine vinegar
4 large egg whites
225g white caster sugar

Filling

300ml double cream
150g dark chocolate
500g mixed summer berries
 (a good mix of strawberries,
 raspberries, blackcurrants,
 redcurrants, blueberries –
 the choice is yours)
2 or 3 satsumas, peeled
 and segmented
1 tablespoon kirsch (optional)

1. Preheat the oven to 180°C/160°C fan/gas mark 4 and line
   a large baking sheet with greaseproof paper.

2. Mix the cornflour and white wine vinegar to make a paste.
   Whisk the egg whites in a large bowl until they form soft
   peaks. Then, while continuing to whisk, start to gradually add
   the sugar, a spoonful at a time, followed by the cornflour paste,
   until the mixture forms stiff peaks and is smooth and glossy.

3. Spoon the meringue mixture gently on to your prepared
   baking sheet to form a large oblong/basket shape, making sure
   the sides of the meringue basket are built up slightly so that
   the filling will sit inside.

4. Place the meringue in the oven and immediately turn
   the temperature down to 170°C/150°C fan/gas mark 3½.
   Cook for about an hour – the meringue should be light beige
   in colour and crisp to touch on the outside. When it's done,
   turn the oven off but leave the meringue in there to gradually
   cool down – by cooling it slowly you'll get a lovely gooey
   centre to it.

5. While your meringue is cooling, prepare the filling.
    Put the double cream into a large bowl. Break most of
    the dark chocolate into pieces (keep back a square or two
    for decoration) and melt it slowly in a bowl over a pan of
    simmering water. Once melted, let the chocolate cool
    slightly for a few minutes and then add it to the double
    cream. Whip the cream and chocolate until the mixture
    thickens and forms soft peaks – it should be fairly thick
    but you want it to still be creamy and luscious.

6. Next, prepare the fruit. Put all the fruit into a large bowl,
    including the peeled and segmented satsumas, and stir in
    the kirsch so that all the fruit gets a little drink! You don't
    have to add kirsch if you prefer not to, but I think it plumps
    up the fruit and enhances the flavour.

7. When the meringue has completely cooled, spoon in the
    chocolate cream mixture and tumble the fruits on top – the
    less precise the better here, as you want to make it look like
    the berries have been gathered straight from the forest and
    tumbled into a basket. Grate a little bit of dark chocolate on
    top and chill in the fridge until you're ready to eat. Serve as
    is, or with chocolate sauce or single cream.

Big Bad's Simple Vanilla Cakes

Poor old Big Bad Wolf – he rather met his match when he came up against the woodcutter, didn't he? After bonneting up and devouring Grandma and Little Red Riding Hood, his tummy was so full he couldn't help but have a nap and thus he fell foul to the woodsman's sharp and shiny axe. Fortunately for Big Bad it was a clean cut, and a hundred stitches down his belly later, he was on the road to recovery. He's learnt his lesson, mind you; rather than stalking the woods for his next meal, these days he's more content with scouring his cupboards for ingredients and whipping up a cake or two. However, not being a natural born baker, it's taken the Big Bad Wolf a little time to master the art, so he started with something straightforward – this recipe for iced vanilla cupcakes. A simple but perfect teatime treat!

MAKES 12

Cake batter

110g softened unsalted butter

110g caster sugar

2 large eggs

2 tablespoons milk

1 teaspoon vanilla extract

110g self-raising flour, sifted

1 teaspoon baking powder

Icing

60g unsalted butter

250g icing sugar – sieved

1 tablespoon milk

½ teaspoon vanilla extract

To decorate

fresh strawberries or
    raspberries (optional)

1. Preheat the oven to 190°C/170°C/gas mark 5 and fill a 12-hole muffin tray with paper muffin cases.

2. Cream the butter and caster sugar together until pale and fluffy, then add the eggs one at a time, mixing well. Add the milk and vanilla extract and mix well.

3. Sift the flour and baking powder and add to the mixture a third at a time, mixing well to ensure that all the dry and wet ingredients are combined.

4. Spoon the mixture into the prepared muffin tray, filling the paper cases about two-thirds full. Place in the centre of the oven and bake for about 20–25 minutes, until the cakes are golden brown, springy to touch, or a skewer comes out clean.

5. Place the cakes to cool on a wire rack.

6. While they are cooling, make the vanilla buttercream icing. Place the softened butter in a large bowl and whip it up, using an electric hand mixer. Add the icing sugar a bit at a time and cream it together with the butter. Add the milk and vanilla extract and mix well until you are left with a smooth, thick creamy icing.

7. When the cakes have cooled completely, pipe or spread the icing on top and decorate as you wish. I like to add a slice of fresh strawberry or a raspberry on top of each cake – the fruit tastes wonderful with the simple vanilla icing and they look stunning.

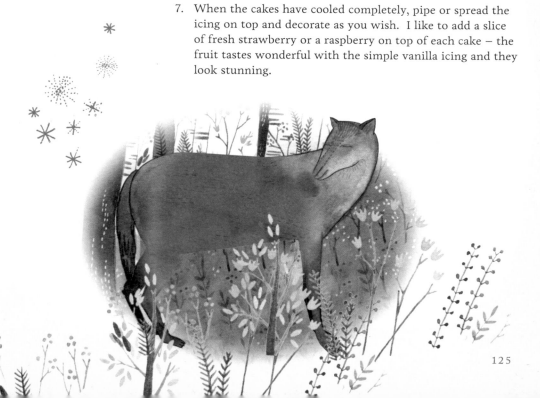

Not
A
TEDDY
BEAR'S
Picnic

Daddy Bear's Big Breakfast Banana Bread

Mummy Bear's Blue and Black Beary Crumble

Baby Bear's Just Right Flapjack

Goldi's Hot Pink Peach Cakes

'Enjoyed a very
pleasant breakfast
with the Three
Bears; Mummy
Bear is just
delightful, I'm sure
we'll remain very
good friends.'

Daddy Bear's Big Breakfast Banana Bread

Of the three bears, Daddy Bear is the biggest. He has the biggest bed, the biggest chair and, naturally, the biggest and sweetest bowl of porridge! So, if you're like Daddy Bear and are partial to scoffing something on the sweeter side for your breakfast, try this lightly spiced, moist banana bread – a great alternative to the usual muffin or croissant. It's the perfect start to any bear's day!

SERVES 8–10

110g softened unsalted butter
150g caster sugar
2 large eggs
2 tablespoons milk
2 tablespoons runny honey
225g self-raising flour, sifted
1 teaspoon baking powder
1 teaspoon mixed spice
2 very ripe large bananas

1. Preheat the oven to 180°C/160°C fan/gas mark 4 and grease a 1kg loaf tin with a little butter.

2. Cream the butter and sugar together in a large bowl until light and fluffy, then add the eggs one at a time, mixing well. Add the milk and honey and mix well.

3. Add the flour, along with the baking powder and mixed spice, and stir well. Finally, mash up the bananas and add them to the cake batter, mixing well.

4. Pour the mixture into your prepared loaf tin and bake for around 50 minutes to 1 hour, until the cake is well risen, just firm on top and a skewer comes out clean.

5. Leave the cake in the tin to cool for a few minutes before turning it out on to a wire rack to cool completely.

6. Lastly, cut yourself a thick slice, grab a big mug of coffee and scoff away!

Mummy Bear's Blue and Black Beary Crumble

I discovered that Mummy Bear and I actually have quite a lot in common aside from our mutual love of cooking. She is extremely house-proud, enjoys a good brisk stroll through the woods, adores any sort of shopping and achieves maximum contentment when she's curled up on the sofa in her pyjamas, tucking into some pudding while watching Strictly Come Dancing! *And if all that sounds rather tempting (I'm pulling on my PJ bottoms as I write), grab the remote, get a spoon and tuck into a bowlful of her delightful crumble. Brimming with juicy blueberries and tangy blackberries, it's the perfect pudding to snuggle up with. Oh, and whatever you do, don't forget the custard!*

SERVES 4

Filling

a little butter, for greasing
300g fresh blueberries
300g fresh blackberries
   (if you can't get fresh you can
   use frozen, but thoroughly
   defrost them first)
1 large Bramley cooking apple,
   cored, peeled and cut into
   small chunks
50g caster sugar
juice of ½ a lemon

Crumble topping

200g self-raising flour, sifted
150g cold unsalted butter,
   cut into small cubes
150g caster sugar

1. Preheat the oven to 190°C/170°C fan/gas mark 5 and lightly grease an ovenproof baking dish (approximately 30 x 21 x 6cm) with a little unsalted butter.

2. To make the fruity filling, place all the fruit, along with the caster sugar and lemon juice, in a non-stick pan and cook on a medium heat for about 15–20 minutes, until the fruit has softened and released its juices. Once cooked, put the filling into the prepared baking dish and leave to one side to cool down a little while you make the crumble topping.

3. Put the flour and butter into a large bowl and, using your hands, rub the butter into the flour – just like you would do if you were making pastry – until the mixture resembles breadcrumbs. Stir in the caster sugar and mix well.

4. Spoon the crumble topping over the top of the fruit and place in the oven for about 35–45 minutes, until the topping is golden brown.

5. Serve nice and warm, with lashings of custard or a big dollop of cream.

Baby Bear's Just Right Flapjack

Dear, sweet, innocent little Baby Bear – he's a cute one, isn't he! But he can also be pretty fussy and picky when he wants to be. Everything has to be just right and he won't stand for anything less, which I think we can all relate to sometimes. For me it's cushions; I cannot stand it if one is out of place, upside down or back to front – honestly, it makes me slightly crazed! Anyhow, as a result of his 'perfectionism', Baby Bear is becoming quite a competent little cook and is keen to help Mummy Bear and Daddy Bear in the kitchen whenever he can. One of his favourite things to make is flapjack; he loves the stuff and can't get enough of its sticky, syrupy, golden goodness. Add some chunks of chocolate and some sultanas to the mix and here is his recipe – I shan't say it's perfection, but to me, it's all right!

MAKES 12
200g unsalted butter,
  plus a little for greasing
375g porridge oats
75g sultanas
a pinch of salt
75g Demerara sugar
100g golden syrup
100g milk chocolate chips

1. Preheat the oven to 180°C/160°C fan/gas mark 4 and grease a 23cm square baking tin with a little butter.

2. Place the oats, sultanas and salt in a large mixing bowl, stir and leave to one side.

3. Put the butter, sugar and syrup into a non-stick pan over a low-medium heat and stir well until melted. Pour this mixture over the oats and mix well, ensuring that all the oats are covered.

4. Stir in the chocolate chips, making sure they are evenly distributed throughout, then tip into the prepared baking tin. Press the mixture down firmly into the prepared tin and level the top with the back of a spoon.

5. Bake in the oven for about 30–35 minutes, until the flapjack is golden brown.

6. Leave to cool for about 15 minutes, then take a knife and mark 12 squares on the top of the flapjack. Leave to cool in the tin completely before cutting out the squares. Store in an airtight container.

7. Sweet and moreish, these flapjacks are a delicious and naughty afternoon treat!

Goldi's Hot Pink Peach Cakes

If I'm honest, before I met Goldilocks I wasn't entirely sure what to make of her. I'd always had her down as a bit of a troublemaker and assumed the worst, like most of us would; after all, she did just waltz into the Three Bears' cottage while they were out, eat their breakfast, break their furniture and sleep in their beds. But when I sat down with Goldi in her local café for a cup of mint tea and a bun, I was pleasantly surprised. Yes, she was cheeky, yes, she was a little mischievous, and yes, she did manage to break a chair (don't ask me how), and OK, I suspect she might have pocketed a scone on the way out. But on the whole she was a sweet, pretty, lovely young lady with adventure pulsing through her veins, and for me, these hot pink peach cakes are the perfect homage to Miss Locks. Filled with a warming, fruity peach and ginger compote and topped with a bright and brazen fuchsia icing, these little pink cupcakes really are hot stuff!

Makes 12

Cake batter
110g softened unsalted butter
110g caster sugar
2 large eggs
2 tablespoons milk
½ teaspoon vanilla extract
110g self-raising flour, sifted
1 teaspoon baking powder
½ teaspoon mixed spice

Filling
120g peach conserve
  (I use Wilkin and Sons,
  as it's full of little chunks
  of peach)
grated zest of 1 lemon
5g fresh ginger, peeled
  and grated
½ tablespoon lemon juice

1. Preheat the oven to 180°C/160°C fan/gas mark 4 and fill a 12-hole muffin tray with paper muffin cases.

2. Cream the butter and caster sugar together until pale and fluffy, then add the eggs one at a time, mixing well. Add the milk and vanilla extract and mix well.

3. Mix the flour, baking powder and mixed spice in a bowl and add to the mixture a third at a time, mixing well to ensure that all the dry and wet ingredients are combined.

4. Spoon the mixture into the prepared muffin tray, filling the paper cases about two-thirds full. Place in the centre of the oven and bake for about 20–25 minutes, until they are golden brown, springy to touch, or a skewer comes out clean.

5. Place the cakes to cool on a wire rack and while they are cooling, prepare the filling and make the icing.

6. For the filling, put the peach conserve into a small non-stick pan with the grated lemon zest, ginger and lemon juice, and cook on a medium heat for about 5 minutes, until the conserve has melted down a little. Take off the heat and leave to one side to cool completely.

Icing

60g unsalted butter
250g icing sugar, sifted
2 tablespoons milk
½ teaspoon vanilla extract
¼ teaspoon pink food
    colouring paste

To decorate

gold edible glitter (optional)
slices of fresh peach (optional)

7. To make the icing, put the softened butter into a large bowl and whip it up, using an electric hand mixer. Add the icing sugar a bit at a time and cream it with the butter. Next add the milk, vanilla extract and pink food colouring and mix well until you have smooth and creamy pink icing – I try to aim for a hot fuchsia shade of pink, not the pale rose variety!

8. Once the cakes are cooled, angle a small sharp knife and cut a round out of the middle of each cake, leaving a hole in the centre. Fill the centre of each cake with a teaspoon or so of the peach mixture, place the piece of sponge back in the cake to plug the hole, and either spread or pipe the icing on top.

9. Finally, decorate as you wish, but I always add a sprinkling of edible glitter (I use gold as it looks so glamorous against the hot pink). I sometimes add a slice of fresh peach on top, but remember to do this just before you are going to serve the cakes.

WONDERLAND

Alice's Amaretto Cakes

Queen of Hearts Pudding

White Rabbit's Speedy Syllabub

The Mad Hatter's Teacakes

'The Queen of Hearts had an almighty
row with the Mad Hatter, she threatened
to cut off his head – I left at that point.'

Alice's Amaretto Cakes ♥

Alice, bless her little stripy tights, is regarded by most of us these days as something of an icon. She's young, striking, fearless, intelligent and witty, and an all-round decent role model for us girls. Of course, I wouldn't actively encourage anyone to start plummeting down rabbit holes or strike up a conversation with a smoking caterpillar, but I do think there's something to be said for having an adventurous spirit! I mean, life without a little bit of mystery and freedom would be very dull indeed, wouldn't it? Alice certainly wouldn't be the Alice we all know and love if all she did was study and play in the garden with her cat. My adventures are of course with food, and for me, any sort of culinary restriction results in sheer and utter panic. In particular, the mere thought of a life without a slightly boozy, cherry cupcake would be close to disastrous, so it's just as well that Alice's inspirational recipe for these glorious Amaretto-soaked cakes is ever present. Phew, major disaster averted!

MAKES 12

Cake batter

80g glacé cherries, chopped into small pieces, washed and dried
110g self-raising flour, sifted
110g softened unsalted butter
110g caster sugar
2 large eggs
2 tablespoons milk
1 teaspoon almond essence
1 teaspoon baking powder
1½ tablespoons Amaretto (to soak into the cakes once they are cooked)

Icing

60g unsalted butter
250g icing sugar, sifted
1 tablespoon milk
1 tablespoon Amaretto

1. Preheat the oven to 190°C/170°C fan/gas mark 5 and fill a 12-hole muffin tray with paper muffin cases.

2. Chop, wash and dry the glacé cherries, then toss them in a little flour and set to one side.

3. Cream the butter and caster sugar together until pale and fluffy, then add the eggs one at a time, mixing well. Add the milk and almond essence and mix well.

4. Sift the flour and baking powder into a bowl and add to the mixture a third at a time, mixing well to ensure that all the dry and wet ingredients are combined, then gently stir in the cherries.

5. Spoon the mixture into the prepared muffin tray, filling the paper cases about two-thirds full. Place in the centre of the oven and bake for about 20–25 minutes, until the cakes are golden brown, springy to touch, or a skewer comes out clean.

To decorate
silver edible glitter or pink
 sugar strands (optional)

TIP

Don't worry if your cherries sink
 to the bottom of your cupcakes.
 Washing and drying them and
 tossing them in flour should help
 prevent this, but it's not the end
 of the world if they plummet like
 Alice down the rabbit hole – your
 cakes will still taste delicious!

6. Place them to cool on a wire rack and spoon a little Amaretto over each one so that it soaks into the sponge.

7. While the cakes are cooling, make the buttercream icing. Place the softened butter in a large bowl and whip it up, using an electric hand mixer. Add the icing sugar a bit at a time and cream it together with the butter. Next add the milk and Amaretto and mix well until you have a smooth, thick creamy icing.

8. When the cakes have cooled completely, pipe or spread the icing on top of each one and decorate as you wish. I think a dusting of silver edible glitter; a cherry or some pink sugar strands look really pretty.

Queen of Hearts Pudding ♥

Although the Mad Hatter had warned me about just how frightening the Queen of Hearts was, I didn't really take him that seriously. Well, would you? He is mad, after all. Needless to say, I should have listened to him. She was petrifying! I'd walked up to the palace gates and was waiting patiently by one of her beautiful rose bushes, when I heard her coming. There was a brief fanfare of trumpets and before I knew it, she had rounded the corner and was standing right in front of me. She glared menacingly, studying me for a moment, but then her face softened a little and I even think she may have smiled as she uttered those now infamous words: 'Off with her head!' Now I don't know what you would have done in such a situation, but I'd travelled a long way, I was tired, hungry and I couldn't be bothered to fight with the woman, so I agreed to have my head offed as long as I was granted one final request – to have dinner with Her Majesty. To my surprise, and huge relief, the Queen agreed and we were soon sitting down to a glorious royal supper.

When it was time for pudding I was naturally starting to get a bit nervous, so I set out to charm the Queen with stories from my travels around Fairytale Land and do you know, it worked. She was soon chatting away, and in between mouthfuls of her delicious cherry Queen of Puddings, she told me of her love for croquet, explained why she is constantly irritated by the Mad Hatter and how she very occasionally likes to wander around her garden tending to her roses. However, before long our bowls were clear and there I was, waiting for my head to roll. But the Queen was so content after having such a nice girly chat and a big dollop of dessert that she kindly decided to let me go, as long as I promised to include her favourite pudding recipe in my book. So, as I wish to remain fully intact, it's all yours, my lovelies!

a knob of unsalted butter
500ml whole milk
1 teaspoon vanilla extract
¼ teaspoon grated nutmeg
25g golden caster sugar
100g white breadcrumbs
2 large eggs, separated
2 x 425g tins of pitted black
  cherries, drained
2 tablespoons kirsch
1 teaspoon granulated sugar
25g white caster sugar,
  for the meringue

1. Preheat the oven to 200°C/180°C fan/gas mark 6 and grease an ovenproof dish (approximately 30 x 21 x 6cm) with a little unsalted butter.

2. Put the milk, vanilla and nutmeg into a pan over a low heat until the milk starts to boil. Remove from the heat and add the golden caster sugar and the breadcrumbs. Put to one side and leave to cool down for about 30 minutes.

3. When the mixture has cooled, add the 2 egg yolks, stir well, and pour into the prepared dish. Place in the oven and bake for about 30 minutes, until the custard/breadcrumb mix has set. Remove from the oven and leave to one side.

4. Put the drained cherries into a small non-stick pan with the kirsch and granulated sugar and cook on a medium heat for about 10 minutes, breaking the fruit up with a spoon so that it is mashed up. Spread the cherry mixture over the baked custard.

5. Finally, make the meringue topping: whisk the egg whites until they form stiff peaks, then whisk in the white caster sugar until the meringue mixture is glossy. Spoon the meringue on top of the cherry layer and return the dish to the oven for a further 10 minutes or so, until golden brown.

6. Serve warm – with some single cream if you're feeling royally wicked!

White Rabbit's Speedy Syllabub ♥

The White Rabbit is one heck of a busy bunny to track down, I can tell you. He's always on the move and rarely has a moment to spare. If he's not rushing off to his next meeting, I can guarantee you'll see him dressed to the nines in his little tweed waistcoat, pacing the room, eyes fixed on his dainty pocket-watch until it's time for him to leave. Hmmm, sound like a familiar experience to anyone? But even though time is very much of the essence to Mr W. Rabbit, food is important to him too, and over the years he has learnt to cook up some delicious dishes in the blink of an eye. This simple strawberry syllabub is one of his favourite desserts; I promise you, it's so swift and easy to make you'll never be late for a date again!

MAKES 4

300g fresh strawberries
50g caster sugar
300ml double cream
zest of 1 lemon
2 tablespoons rum
  (preferably golden)

'Oh dear! Oh dear!
I shall be too late.'

1. Take half the strawberries, remove the stalks, cut them in half and put them into a bowl. Add the sugar, then, using a fork, crush the strawberries and sugar together so that they are mashed up and release their lovely juices.

2. Put the cream, lemon zest and rum into a separate bowl and whisk until the cream thickens to form soft peaks. Add the mashed strawberries and fold in well, making sure the fruit is evenly dispersed among the cream.

3. Set aside a couple of the remaining strawberries for decoration and slice up the rest, making sure you remove the stalks. Take your dessert dishes (I sometimes use small wine glasses) and line the base and sides with a layer of the sliced strawberries, taking them between a third and halfway up the sides. Carefully spoon in the syllabub, then slice the reserved strawberries and place a couple of slices on top of each one.

4. Place the syllabubs in the fridge for an hour or two to chill thoroughly before serving. These are delicious eaten just as they are, but you could serve them with some amaretti biscuits on the side for dipping if you like!

The Mad Hatter's Teacakes ♥

Now where else would I find the Mad Hatter but at his very own tea party, and what a tea party it was. The long, white-linen-covered table was so abundantly adorned with crowded cake-stands, jam-packed pudding dishes and steaming teapots that I could barely see from one end to the other. I really had to squint to spot the dear little dormouse; he was curled up so very tightly inside a tiny teapot! Anyway, as you can imagine, taking tea with the Hatter was a slightly maddening experience, as it involved rather a lot of tea and far too much chit-chat; something about ravens, writing desks and butter . . . oh, who knows? But, to give him his due, the Hatter, however barmy, knows how to bake a good cake, and this recipe for 'teacakes' was his parting gift to me. Full of juicy sultanas and topped with a delicate cinnamon butter cream, these tea-laced cupcakes will turn your taste buds doolally!

MAKES 12

Cake batter

100ml strong tea
  (use 2 teabags)
100g sultanas
110g softened unsalted butter
110g caster sugar
2 large eggs
1 tablespoon milk
110g self-raising flour, sifted
1 teaspoon mixed spice
1 teaspoon baking powder

Icing

60g unsalted butter
250g icing sugar, sifted
½ teaspoon ground cinnamon
2 tablespoons milk
¼ teaspoon vanilla extract

1. Preheat the oven to 190°C/170°C fan/gas mark 5 and fill a 12-hole muffin tray with paper muffin cases.

2. In a jug, make your tea and brew for about 5 minutes. Remove the tea bags, then put the sultanas into the tea and leave them to soak while the tea cools.

3. Cream the butter and caster sugar together until pale and fluffy, then add the eggs one at a time, mixing well. Add the milk.

4. Sift the flour, mixed spice and baking powder into a bowl and add to the mixture a third at a time, mixing well to ensure that all the dry and wet ingredients are combined. Lastly, stir in the cooled tea and soaked sultanas.

5. Spoon the mixture into the prepared muffin tray, filling the paper cases about two-thirds full. Place in the centre of the oven and bake for about 20–25 minutes, until the cakes are springy to touch, or a skewer comes out clean. Leave them to cool on a wire rack.

To decorate
gold edible glitter (optional)
white sugar flowers (optional)

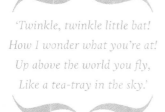

'Twinkle, twinkle little bat!
How I wonder what you're at!
Up above the world you fly,
Like a tea-tray in the sky.'

6. While the cakes are cooling, make the buttercream icing. Put the softened butter into a large bowl and whip it, using an electric hand mixer. Add the icing sugar a bit at a time and cream it together with the butter. Next add the cinnamon, milk and vanilla and mix well until you have a smooth, thick, creamy icing.

7. When the cakes have cooled completely, pipe or spread the icing on top of each one and decorate as you wish. I like to add a tiny dusting of gold edible glitter and a little white sugar flower to the top of each cake.

8. Serve at any sophisticated tea party, with a nice hot cup of tea.

DAMSELS
and
DRAGONS

Dragon-Fire Chilli

Fair Maiden Guacamole

My Hero's Hot Bananas

'Met my hero today;
what a man! They don't
make them like that
very often!'

Dragon-Fire Chilli

A long time ago, a young and reckless knight thought it would be amusing to call his grandmother 'The Dragon'. Thanks to the vicious disposition of this old crone, dragons throughout the land have since been branded as brutal and ferocious beasts. Of course, I can't deny the fact that these gigantic fire-breathing winged monsters with sharp claws, scaly skin and huge serpent-like tails have a tendency to burn down houses and munch on the odd person or cow here and there, but I hope you won't be swayed by all this bad press. I urge you to see these glorious creatures for what they truly are: rather large flying lizards with a love of very spicy food. Where did you think all that fire came from? This fiery chilli pays homage to all the hot-headed dragons of old.

SERVES 2–4

1 tablespoon olive oil,
   for frying
500g minced beef
1 red onion, finely chopped
1 teaspoon
   Worcestershire sauce
3 chillies – 1 green, 2 red,
   seeded and finely chopped
½ teaspoon dried chilli flakes
½ teaspoon paprika
½ teaspoon cayenne pepper
½ teaspoon ground coriander
1 x 420g tin of kidney beans,
   drained and rinsed
1 x 400g tin of
   chopped tomatoes
2 teaspoons tomato purée
salt and freshly ground
   black pepper
juice of 1 lime
a handful of fresh coriander,
   roughly chopped

1. Heat the olive oil in a large pan (preferably non-stick), then add the mince and fry until browned – this should take about 5 minutes on a moderately high heat.

2. Add the onions and continue cooking until they start to soften. Add the Worcestershire sauce.

3. Next, add the chillies (fresh and dried), followed by the paprika, cayenne pepper and ground coriander, and stir well.

4. Add the kidney beans, tomatoes and tomato purée and season well with salt and pepper. You'll need to add a little more liquid to the chilli at this point so that it doesn't dry out, so fill your empty tomato can half full with water and add to the pan. Add half the lime juice at this point.

5. Bring the chilli to the boil, then turn the heat right down low so that it can simmer very gently for a good couple of hours until the sauce has reduced down. You don't need to cover it with a lid, but if you've got a splash guard that's a good option.

6. Once cooked, stir in the fresh coriander and add the last of the lime juice to give it a final zesty kick. Serve with long-grain rice or tacos and my Fair Maiden Guacamole.

TIP

I use 3 fresh chillies and a sprinkling of dried chilli flakes in this recipe, but if you can't take the heat and prefer to avoid the wrath of the dragon, reduce the amount of chilli to suit you. Likewise, if you're a chilli fiend, increase the amount of chillies or just add Tabasco sauce to taste when the chilli is cooked.

Fair Maiden Guacamole

As fair maidens we often find ourselves at the mercy of dragons and other perils: boyfriends, girlfriends, spots, chipped nail varnish, split ends, feeling over-emotional . . . and after all that we need something mouth-wateringly tasty to calm us down. This delicious homemade guacamole sacrifices itself wonderfully to the heady heat of my Dragon-fire Chilli, but you can also serve it with fajitas or as a dip with some tortilla chips.

SERVES 2–4

1 large ripe avocado

2–3 spring onions, finely chopped

2 tomatoes, seeded and finely chopped

¼ teaspoon dried chilli flakes

a small handful of fresh coriander, roughly chopped

juice of ½ a lemon

salt and ground white pepper

1. Peel the avocado and remove the stone – hold on to the stone, though, as you'll need it later on.

2. In a bowl, mash the avocado flesh with a fork – it doesn't have to be smooth, and in fact I think it's better when it has some texture to it.

3. Add the rest of the ingredients and stir well, seasoning to taste – the avocado can take a fair amount of salt.

4. If you're not going to eat the guacamole straight away, put the avocado stone back into the guacamole until you're ready to serve it – this will prevent the mixture from discolouring.

My Hero's Hot Bananas

I first met my hero in a pub, which I believe is where most of us maidens meet our heroes these days. Through a haze of ale and pork scratchings I saw him standing there, all muscles, with his sword and shield at his side, propped up against the bar making eyes at the serving wench. Typical! Of course, like any maiden I like a challenge; so with a flick of my hair and a twinkle in my eye, I walked straight up to this Adonis of a man and asked if I could buy him a pint. After the usual bout of uncertainty and relationship analysis, the rest is . . . well, history. In addition to being ridiculously handsome and excellent at hero-ing, I also discovered he had a knack for making a rather delicious hot, fudgy banana pudding. Believe me, ladies; it will make your knees wobble and your heart flutter . . .

SERVES 2

a little butter or oil,
  for greasing
4–5 large ripe bananas
  (you need approx. 2 large
  bananas per person)
4 tablespoons soft dark sugar
1 tablespoon dark rum
approx. 50ml double cream
  (you need enough to only
  just cover the bananas)

1. Preheat the oven to 220°C/200°C fan/gas mark 7 and grease a shallow baking dish with a little butter or oil.

2. Peel the bananas, cut them into quarters (first cut them in half lengthways, then halve each piece crossways), and place them in the bottom of the prepared dish.

3. Sprinkle over about 3 tablespoons of the sugar and the rum.

4. Place in the oven and cook for 5–10 minutes, until the bananas have softened and the sugar and rum have melted and begun to caramelise.

5. Remove from the oven and preheat the grill to its hottest temperature.

6. Spoon the double cream over the bananas; you want it to just cover them. Sprinkle the remaining sugar on top.

7. Place under the grill and cook for about another 5 minutes – the cream will start to thicken and turn fudgy as it cooks with the sugar. You want the sugar to caramelise and the top to brown without burning.

8. When ready, remove from the oven and serve with vanilla or chocolate ice-cream – or both!

To My Hero,

As I sit here at my kitchen table, writing my declaration of the eternal crush I have on you, part of me thinks that I will never send you this letter. I will just chicken out. I will just fold it up and hide it away with my tights. I will deny all knowledge. It will be easier that way. But then the other part of my 'bedazzled by you' brain thinks what the heck, I must tell you how I feel. We had such a great time last week and I'm so glad that I summoned the courage to buy you a drink. Of course, you have various wenches and eyelash-fluttering floozies falling at your feet the whole time and you can have your pick of any of them, but I do hope I'm a contender.

If you don't reciprocate my feelings then that's 'fine', I'll be OK, I'll be a little embarrassed perhaps, slightly red of cheek, but ultimately I'll be all right. And of course, it goes without saying that I'll completely understand if you just want to be friends . . .

Actually, no, scrap that! No! I won't be OK. I'll be devastated if you don't like me. I'll hate it. I'll be a snivelling mess. I will bawl my eyes out and eat cake until my tummy hurts, because I adore you. I know this all sounds so clichéd and hideously desperate and I'm sorry for ranting. It's just that every time I see you walk into the pub I melt. Every time you speak to me with those runny-honey tones of yours, I want to run away with you to a magical faraway place. Every time you swing your sword and brandish that tonne-heavy shield of yours and I see your biceps bulging, I just know you are the man for me.

Anyway, I hope you don't mind me writing this down. You probably think I'm mad or deluded, or both. And even if I am, both, there is one more thing that I definitely am . . . completely, utterly and unashamedly in love with you and all I really wanted to ask is that I hope you love me too? x

Enchanted Essentials

Here, in my opinion, are the key ingredients and utensils that every fairytale cook should have in their kitchen (which is thoroughly goblin-proofed of course) . . .

GENERAL INGREDIENTS

Olive oil
Use good-quality olive oil. Milder flavoured oils are good for frying, while extra virgin is perfect for salad dressings and dips.

Herbs and spices
I use both fresh and dried herbs and spices. Here are the ones I use most often: parsley, basil, mint, coriander, chives, thyme, rosemary, bay leaves, sage, paprika, cayenne pepper, chilli flakes, cinnamon, ginger, mixed spice, nutmeg and cardamom pods.

Stock
I love making my own stock when I have the time, but I also use shop-bought liquid stock or stock cubes.

Mushroom ketchup
Geo Watkins Mushroom Ketchup is one of my all-time favourite ingredients and I urge you to go out and buy a bottle right now. It adds such a flavoursome depth to soups, stews and sauces – I just love it!

Double cream
Cream often plays a major role in my pudding making, but it also has its savoury uses in soups, sauces and quiches.

BAKING INGREDIENTS

Flour
It's worth having plenty of plain and self-raising flour stashed away in your cupboards, so that if you suddenly fancy baking some cupcakes, biscuits, scones, pastry or pancakes, you can!

Butter
My fridge is constantly filled with packs of butter. Use unsalted butter in baking unless the recipe states that you should use salted. I take the butter out of the fridge about an hour or so before I begin to bake, so that it is nicely softened by the time I start. If you have a microwave you can ping the butter for a few seconds to soften it, but just make sure it doesn't melt!

Caster sugar
Golden caster sugar is great to use when making cupcakes and biscuits, but I always use white caster sugar when making meringues, as it ensures that they turn a gloriously snowy white.

Eggs
Use large, preferably free-range eggs unless otherwise stated. Make sure they are at room temperature before you use them.

Chocolate
Always use good-quality chocolate – a chocolate with 70% cocoa content is usually recommended for cooking.

Flavourings, colourings and decorations
Vanilla extract is THE most important extract to have in your store cupboard as far as I'm concerned. You will use it endlessly when making cakes and puddings, so it is worth

investing in a good-quality extract, as you'll get a much better flavour. You can of course buy vanilla pods, but they are quite expensive, so I only use them occasionally. The other extracts and flavourings I would recommend are French almond, lemon and rosewater.

Use food colouring pastes rather than the little bottles of colouring liquid. Pastes produce a much more vibrant colour and you only need to add a teeny, tiny amount to achieve the colour you desire.

Decorations literally come in all shapes, colours, and sizes, from sugar sprinkles, shiny dragees and chocolate buttons to sugar flowers and edible glitter; there are so many out there to choose from.

UTENSILS

Whiz it, chop it, blend it

I use both a hand whisk and an electric whisk. A hand whisk is great for more delicate whipping jobs, but I'll always use an electric whisk for those more arm-ache-inducing whips like creaming butter and sugar and making meringues.

A food processor or a mini food chopper/blender is a really useful piece of cooking kit. These have many different functions but I mostly use mine for finely chopping vegetables, mincing meat, making breadcrumbs and blending soups.

Pans, dishes and tins

Over the years I have managed to accumulate loads of pans, dishes, tins and trays for general cooking and baking. You don't necessarily need to have all of the below but these are the types and sizes used throughout the book.

Pans – a selection of saucepans and a frying pan – some preferably non-stick
Casserole dish – one that can be used on the hob and in the oven
Ovenproof dish approx. 30 x 21 x 6cm
Large roasting dish or tray
23cm flan dish
20cm round cake tin x 2
23cm diameter, 7cm deep round spring-form cake tin
23cm square baking tin
12-hole muffin tray
12-hole mini muffin tray x 2
1kg loaf tin
Large baking sheets, preferably non-stick
Disposable foil roasting tray (29.8 x 23.5 x 3.8 cm)
Ramekins or dessert dishes

Bits and bobs

Mixing bowls – good to have a selection; I have small, medium and large
Jelly mould – I have a 570ml plastic mould
Ice lolly moulds – I use a Faringdon Ice Lolly Mould
Wooden spoons
Spatula
Palette knife
Icing nozzles and piping bag/s
Wooden or metal skewer – great for testing cakes, and for kebabs of course!
Cooling rack
Airtight storage containers

Suppliers

MEAT, POULTRY AND GAME
Macken Brothers Ltd
44 Turnham Green Terrace, London W4 1QP
Tel: 020 8994 2646

FISH AND SEAFOOD
Covent Garden Fishmongers
37 Turnham Green Terrace, London W4 1RG
Tel: 020 8995 9273

FRUIT AND VEG
Andreas Fine Fruit and Vegetables
35 Turnham Green Terrace, London W4 1RG
Tel: 020 8995 0140

GENERAL COOKWARE
Whisk Cooking Solutions
1a Devonshire Road, Chiswick, London W4 2EU
Tel: 020 8995 8990

DECORATIONS, COLOUR PASTE, EDIBLE GLITTER AND MORE
Jane Asher Party Cakes and Sugarcraft Shop
22–24 Cale Street, London SW3 3QU
Tel: 020 7584 6177
www.janeasher.com

Cakes, Cookies and Crafts Shop
Tel: 015 2438 9684
www.cakescookiesandcraftsshop.co.uk

Acknowledgements

To Trevor Dolby, Nicola Taplin, Susan Sandon and
Julie Jefferies; thank you for giving me this amazing
opportunity. Having the chance to write *Fairytale Food* has
meant so much to me. It has been incredibly exciting, tiring
and yes, a little bit fattening at times, but I am thrilled that
my book has been published by such a creative, encouraging
and supportive team of people – it couldn't be in safer hands.
I would also like to say a huge thank you to the rest of my
colleagues at Cornerstone. Everyone has been so positive and
supportive and for that I am truly grateful to you all.

Now this book wouldn't be what it is without the stunning
illustrations and design. Many thanks must go to the
wonderfully talented Yelena Bryksenkova whose astoundingly
beautiful illustrations capture my vision of fairytales so
perfectly and to the fabulous designer David Eldridge and
his team, who really have turned this book into a thing
of beauty. It looks truly magical – thank you!

Lastly, I could not have even attempted to write this book
without having the advice, support and love from my family;
Rhys, Mum, Dad, Robert, Gran, Vanessa, Haydn and Roly –
I couldn't have done it without you. x

Index